THE WOMEN IN HIS LIFE: WHAT JESUS SAW IN THEM

BY

PATRICIA DALY

Copyright © 2014 by Patricia Daly

Printed by CreateSpace, An Amazon.com Company

www.PatriciaDalyWrites.com

TABLE OF CONTENTS

Print Edition License Note

THE COVER

Cover Design by www.fiverr.com/vikiana

Two chess pieces appear on the cover, the king and his pawns. My heartfelt thanks are extended to my cousin and soul-sister, Kathleen B. MacMurray, for her explanation of the role of the pawn in chess, which translates perfectly to the relationship between Jesus and the women in his life:

> *"Pawns are warriors! They are the first line of defense and the first to attack. In 'end-game' of Chess, the pawns can also be turned into Queens! Pawns have power! They are often overlooked, or underestimated --- like women throughout history!!! And ......Of course their main objective is to protect the King!"*

And from a book published in 1749: "The pawn is the soul of chess. ... They are the very Life of the Game. They alone form the Attack and the Defense; on their good or bad Situation depends the Gain or Loss of the Party."

François-André Danican Philidor, 1749 (Euwe & Hooper 1959:1).

Dedication and Acknowledgments

For my uncle,
Brother M. Theodore Daly, OCSO
"Uncle Ed"
April 16, 1928 – March 27, 2013

And all my brothers at Abbey of the Genesee, Piffard, New York

Bibles verses are taken from The New American Bible and used in accordance with the publisher's guidelines. Copyright © Catholic Publishers, Inc., 1971. Text of The New American Bible Copyright © Confraternity of Christian Doctrine, 1970

Quote from John 16:21-22, NEW MOM'S JOY: No One Can Take It From You, Contemporary English Version (CEV)

Special thanks to the members of my writing group, *Women of the Roundtable*, for their excellent feedback and suggestions: Jan, Sheila, Pat, Susan, and Heidi. Without their support I would not have gotten to this place.

Thanks to Dr. Gary Wasserman for his clarification concerning the legal status of Jewish women in the 1st Century.

Debra Marrs, www.yourwritelife.com, generously guided me through technological challenges that almost did me in. I am so grateful!

Particular thanks are extended to the following authors whose eBooks on Kindle publishing have been indescribably valuable. They convinced me I could do it:

Steve Scott (www.stevescottsite.com)

Tom Corson-Knowles (www.TCKPublishing.com)

Sean Platt, Johnny B. Truant, with David Wright
(www.amazon.com/Publish-Repeat-No-Luck-Required-Self-Publishing-Success-ebook/dp/B00H26IFJS)

Guy Kawasaki (www.APEthebook.com)

INTRODUCTION: MESSAGE FROM THE AUTHOR

During the summer of 2012 I decided to read through the Gospels of Matthew, Mark, Luke, and John. I had not read either the Old or New Testaments in decades; however, I had returned to a daily practice of spiritual reading and meditation the year before and believed that my spiritual life would be enhanced by including a daily reading from the Gospels. I wanted to rediscover the person of Jesus from a fresh perspective.

The Gospels are rich with nuance and mystery. For centuries biblical scholars have devoted their lives to delving the depths of meaning and implication of every word. It is important and instructive to understand the historical context and original written language to appreciate what the writer is saying. At the same time, the Bible is meant to reveal truth and to guide the reader to an experience of God through prayerful, personal reading. I wanted to read the Gospels for what they revealed in the words I was reading, without input from scholars and commentators.

As I read one Gospel chapter per day, I began to notice interesting tidbits of warmth and caring in Jesus, particularly when a female appeared, either in a parable or in an encounter. I enjoyed seeing through fresh eyes how Jesus related to women. He was at home with them and comfortable. He spoke to them directly and respectfully. Willing to break religious and social rules in their presence, he enjoyed their reactions and responses. He loved the ways in which they managed to maintain their personal dignity in a repressive culture. And he responded from a deep place inside himself when they asked for his help.

More often, women in the New Testament are not the main story, they are the backstory. Even so, they are his joy, his fun, his celebration. It is the women he rejoices in and with, and it is they who stick by him all the way to the end, and beyond death. He knows the depths of a mother's love. He is capable of having female friends. He connects with their unique spark. He recognizes God's beauty, compassion, and loyalty. He recognized himself in their hearts, their love of life, and their devotion to the practical necessities like food, and family, and togetherness.

I was re-introduced to New Testament women we know so well: the mother of Jesus, Mary Magdalen, Peter's mother-in-law, Martha and Mary among them. But I also began to notice others who impacted his life whom he spoke of from his study of the Torah such as the Queen of Sheba and Lot's wife. They receive mention in the Gospels and are important by that fact. They touched the life of Jesus, so they deserve to have their story told through his voice.

As I experienced these things in Jesus, I asked myself, *What was he thinking when he said that?* and *What did he see in her in that situation?* This man, according to the stories I was reading, was healing the sick, the crippled and deformed, blind persons, and the mentally ill. If Jesus really has this power, I concluded, he also must have a tremendous understanding of human nature and the human mind.

The evangelists confirm Jesus' ability to know what was going on in the minds and hearts of the folks he dealt with daily. *But what was going on in **his** mind?* I continued to wonder. *What did he see in **her** that caused him to say what he said, and do what he did?*

I decided to put myself in his place as best I could to look at these women through his eyes, to place myself in the human context of the situation. I imagined what he might be thinking and seeing when he interacted with the personalities in the stories.

Unlike books by scholars who have spent their lives researching and documenting the life and times of famous religious leaders, I claim no theological or educational credentials here. I wrote in today's vernacular as I imagine Jesus might have told these stories if he were sitting down with us. Jesus would have spoken in the vernacular of his own time; if he spoke to us in our own language today, I think he would use words and phrases we ourselves would use and connect with. At times I created a storyline around a woman, and in many places I assigned a name where there was none. I did not capitalize the words him, he, his, me, or my in reference to Jesus.

In the end, all of us have walked in the shoes of many of these individuals at some point in our lives. I'd like to think Jesus sees in us what he saw in them—the best we're made of, and that he wants to draw from us all we're capable of becoming.

I share with you stories of tenderness and appreciation as I imagine them taking place. I hope you will see for yourself a good man and a remarkable human being who defied many religious and cultural expectations and related to women on his own terms, untouched by ego or fear.

HISTORIC AND RELIGIOUS BACKGROUND

When you read the Gospels with a concentration on the interaction between Jesus and women, you appreciate how much he loved, respected and enjoyed them. And then you begin to notice a definite contrast between the men in the Gospels and the women. Jesus often expresses exasperation with the men, including his close followers, as well as with political rulers and Jewish religious leaders. In many Gospel stories you can sense Jesus practicing extraordinary patience in his relationships with the men of his time. There are only two men who are described as being loved by him. They are John, who was one of the twelve disciples, and Lazarus, his friend. Only these two men are presented as eliciting love from Jesus. On the other hand, there are no women in the Gospels who test his patience or disappoint him except the sister-in-law of Herod; and her story is the backdrop to that of her dancing daughter.

Women in the four Gospels appear in a broad variety of settings, ages, and situations. They are mothers, sisters, cousins, friends, servants, wives, neighbors, gentiles and Jews, widows and girls. In their stories they are seen in the roles of grieving mothers, irate widows, intuitives, prostitutes, bridesmaids, cooks, servants, and contemplatives.

Jesus, a balanced, secure and harmonious human being, was male by gender, but he had many traits that we more often associate with women. He was intuitive, emotional, compassionate, caring, forgiving, understanding, insightful, and fiercely loyal to his friends. He truly was a zealot, especially in his treatment of women, and they responded to him because he connected with them through these traits. They recognized that Jesus knew them on a level deeper than physical, and that he related to them personally, despite the social and religious conventions of the time.

Jesus was born in the vast track of Roman-occupicd land encompassing modern-day Israel as well as large parts of Jordan, Syria, and Lebanon.The religious and societal culture in which Jesus was born and raised was not favorable to females. The place and role of women in the first century society was very different from that of our Western culture in the twenty-first century. During Jesus' time, Jewish women were not allowed to speak to or with men in public. They could not testify in court or mingle with men socially. Women generally lived in the shadows; they were uneducated and not expected to contribute to society except within the family.

A Jewish woman had no legal standing except through her connection to her family, her faithfulness to her husband, and her home responsibilities. The laws of inheritance, engagement to be married, and divorce were heavily in favor of men. However, Jewish law did have guidelines in place for the welfare of a woman in cases of the death of a husband or divorce, and for inheritance. After betrothal at an early age, around twelve and a half years old, the father's power over his daughter was transferred to her future husband. The betrothed maiden was already called 'wife.'

Rules of propriety dictated that a man was never to be alone with a woman, nor could he look at a married woman or greet her. Women were discouraged from studying the Torah. They could not teach or speak in the synagogue, nor were they permitted to enter the Court of the Gentiles in the Temple. During worship, women could not receive blessings before and after the Torah reading.

However, in her home a woman was honored, even as she was obligated to perform many household tasks. The family was her true place of belonging and influence in the first century. The Jewish mother was honored and revered equally with the father in the home. The Jewish Talmud instructs a man to love his wife as he loves himself and to respect her more than he respects himself. Jewish mothers of the time were recognized for their spiritual importance; a child was recognized as a Jew by the rabbis only if his mother was a Jewess, no matter what the father's religious leanings were. Also, the rabbis appreciated the power of the woman in the marriage by saying that if a pious man marries an evil woman, he will become evil as well. But if an evil man marries a good woman, she will make him a good man. The power was hers.

This was the religious and cultural formation Jesus received as a Jewish man. Against this backdrop of the male-dominated, patriarchal society, Jesus comes through as a man who honored, appreciated, and responded to the true value and importance of women in society while he was in their presence. He enjoyed their company; he celebrated with them; he was gentle and playful and challenging. He treated women as equals; he honored their natural gifts and disregarded the societal conventions that kept him from interacting with them. He spoke to them directly. He drew from them their opinions and feedback. He saw into their hearts and loved them as unique individuals. He really understood them. And because he did, they responded to him with love, loyalty, and respect.

It is apparent in the Gospels that Jesus had women followers who supported him and his disciples financially; women sheltered and fed them. They followed him all the way to his death on the cross, when every other disciple, except John, was blatantly absent from the scene. He was grateful for their signs of affection, care and

13

concern for him. He was sensitive to their needs, problems and aspirations.

When you consider the unequal role of the woman in the time of Jesus, it is surprising to read the number of times they are mentioned by the four evangelists. Granted, women are portrayed as adulteresses, prostitutes, cripples, foreigners, gentiles and non-Jews, but we are constantly reminded that none of this prevented Jesus from speaking to and ministering to them with respect and heartfelt understanding.

Jesus has been referred to as a zealot. Jesus definitely was radical when it came to his interactions with women and zealous toward them. He was 'enthusiastic, eager, fervid, fervent, intense, passionate, [and] warm' when it came to the women in his life. (Dictionary.com synonyms for zealous) He broke religious and social rules without a second thought of the consequences. Particularly with women, he did not permit the Law of Moses or the rule of Rome to prevent him from ignoring all rules and breaking barriers whenever he related to them. Jesus was a zealot in the most pure sense of the word, especially when it came to the women in his life.

References:

http://www.religioustolerance.org/cfe_bibl.htm

http://wiki.answers.com/Q/What_was_the_place_of_a_women_in_Jewish_society_in_Jesus_time

http://www.bible-history.com/jesus/jesusThe_Role_of_Women.htm

http://www.americancatholic.org/Newsletters/JHP/aq0906.asp

http://au.answers.yahoo.com/question/index?qid=20120322152720

AAvcA3W

http://www.historel.net/english/christ/10femmes.htm

https://bible.org/article/how-jesus-ministered-women

Hawkes, Dennis. *A First-Century Traveller's Guide to Palestine.* Published by Dennis Hawkes at Smashwords, 2012.

A MOTHER'S WORST NIGHTMARE:
LOST CHILD

His parents used to go every year to Jerusalem for the feast of the Passover, and when he was twelve they went up for the celebration as was their custom. As they were returning at the end of the feast, the child Jesus remained behind unknown to his parents. Thinking he was in the party, they continued their journey for a day, looking for him among their relatives and acquaintances. Not finding him, they returned to Jerusalem in search of him. On the third day they came upon him in the temple sitting in the midst of the teachers, listening to them and asking them questions. All who heard him were amazed at his intelligence and his answers. When his parents saw him they were astonished, and his mother said to him: "Son, why have you done this to us? You see that your father and I have been searching for you in sorrow." He said to them: "Why did you search for me? Did you not know I had to be in my Father's house?" But they did not grasp what he said to them. He went down with them then, and came to Nazareth, and was obedient to them. Luke 2:41-51

I could see in her eyes a frantic terror that I had never seen before and would never cause her to direct toward me again. She looked like a prisoner who had been tortured. When she saw me sitting with the Temple teachers, calm and happy, the horror of the experience of a missing child turned into the pain of confusion, caused by the thoughtless behavior that 12-year-olds are so capable of manifesting, especially toward their parents. As our eyes met, my heart sank. I realized she had been heartbroken by my disappearance and I was the cause.

I could see her eyes change from helplessness to hurt as her lips formed the single word, *Why?* In that instant we both knew that the decision I made had caused her to feel the utter agony of a parent of a missing child, an unbearable sense of visceral dissection that would be repeated through the generations and millennia in the hearts of mothers and fathers throughout the world. And then my mother asked me, "Why have you done this to us? See how worried your father and I have been searching for you."

But I was twelve, and defensive. I was not mature enough to accept responsibility for hurting my mother and father, especially unintentionally. They knew I wanted to be around the Temple teachers. They were friends of the Temple official who took me in, who was delighted to have me stay with his family. How was I to know what happens to mothers and fathers when a child disappears? I thought they would figure out I was staying in Jerusalem for a while. That's why I reminded her that I had work to do for my Father in Heaven. "Didn't you know I need to be in my Father's house?" I put the whole situation back on her when I should have been remorseful and apologetic.

And then I could see in her eyes a flash that froze me to my seat. I felt the hairs on my arms rise and my throat closed tight. It was a mother's universal "look" that meant business. I knew enough to say not one more word. I gathered my tablets and went home with my mom and dad. I was confused about what happened so I made up my mind to listen better and do what I was told. Clearly I had screwed up and wasn't about to do anything ever again to deserve that look.

ANNA: GIFT OF PROPHECY

When the eighth day arrived for his circumcision, the name Jesus was given the child, the name the angel had given him before he was conceived. When the day came to purify them according to the law of Moses, the couple brought him up to Jerusalem so that he could be presented to the Lord...There was also [in Jerusalem] a certain prophetess, Anna by name, daughter of Phanuel of the tribe of Asher. She had seen many days, having lived seven years after her husband in marriage and then as a widow until she was eighty-four. She was constantly in the temple, worshiping day and night in fasting and prayer. Coming on the scene at this moment, she gave thanks to God and talked about the child to all who looked forward to the deliverance of Jerusalem. Luke 2:21-22;36-38

I could see in my grandmother her unique pride when she looked at me when I was a child. Her daughter had married a good man and she had given her a grandson to love and spoil. Her life was blessed. She was frequently in our home when I was growing up. She couldn't stay away. Neither could their cousin, Elizabeth, who frequently visited with her son, John. I loved it when they came down from the hill country of Judea. John and I would play as the women talked and talked as they cooked and sewed and washed.

My grandmother, my mother, and their cousin Elizabeth were key women in my upbringing. I learned from them, even when they weren't speaking to me directly. I loved to hear their laughter coming from the kitchen as John and I played.

Although I wasn't interested in their conversations, a name that came up every now and then was Anna. My grandmother's name was Anne, but I called her the Aramaic name for grandmother, *savta*. But they weren't talking about my savta when this Anna was mentioned. She was someone else, someone I did not know. The women would speak in tones of respect and soft whispers when Anna's name came up.

One day, when I was close to eight years old, I asked my grandmother who this Anna was. She gave me her adoring smile that only grandmothers can give. Her eyes met mine; they smiled too. I waited. She was mentally arranging the words an eight-year-old would understand. And then she said,

"Anna was a very holy woman who dedicated her life to Yahweh. She was filled with his Spirit and power. When she spoke, we knew it was Yahweh's truth coming through her. She was very old, the oldest person any of us every saw. She was tiny and wrinkled and bent over, but her voice was filled with powerful energy. Everyone in the land had heard of Anna the Prophetess."

My grandmother paused. She had something else to tell me, but she hesitated. "What else, savta?" I wanted her to keep talking. But the sparkle in her eyes faded. She tried to change the subject, but I wouldn't let it go. "Tell me!" I begged her with the insistence all eight-year-olds possess.

Once more she searched her mind for the right words, words that would not reveal her worry and confusion, but would reveal something to me about myself. When she looked at me again, the smile had returned to her eyes. She took me in her arms and said, "Anna the Prophetess thanked Yahweh for blessing our family with a beautiful son – you – and she said you will someday become a great man in the eyes of Yahweh."

"Wow!" I thought, "That's exciting!" I told my savta that I couldn't wait to grow up and become that great man. She then sent me off to play. When she kissed me, I saw that her eyes were watering. I could not tell if she was happy or sad. It wasn't until I began preaching and caught glimpses of my inevitable death that I thought back to my wise grandmother and knew that she too understood that my life would be painful for me to experience and for others to watch, especially her beloved daughter.

ANNOYING WIDOW: JUSTICE SERVED

He taught them a parable on the necessity of praying always and not losing heart: "Once there was a judge in a certain city who respected neither God nor man. A widow in that city kept coming to him saying, 'Give me my rights against my opponent.' For a time he refused, but finally he thought, 'I care little for God or man, but this widow is wearing me out. I am going to settle in her favor or she will end by doing me violence.'" Luke 18:1-5

Although I never saw her I could hear her. Night after night I heard her. We all did. First she woke us up and then she kept us awake. "She's back again," my father would say as he paced through the house in the darkness.

If she had had a husband he would not have permitted her to carry on like this. But she was a widow with no income and no one to speak up for her.

I was in my 20s when she started her midnight ranting in front of the judge's home. My mother knew Rafca and her story. When Rafca's husband died, his brother took over the business and left his sister-in-law and her children destitute. Rafca took him to court, but the judge would not rule in her favor because he was taking bribes from her brother-in-law.

My mother said, "Don't worry. Rafca will not give up. Every day she asks Yahweh for justice. She has absolute faith that the Lord will help her." My mother had no doubt about Rafca's persistence nor of Yahweh's mercy. "She knows she is right. Her children need to be fed and clothed. You wait and see. Yahweh will come through."

I watched and waited for Yahweh's justice. Every few nights she was back again, calling out the judge's name, calling out her brother-in-law's name, calling out the names of her hungry children. Her voice escalated in intensity and volume as time went by. The sound of her pounding on his door grew louder. She was the talk of the town. And so was the heartless judge.

He was corrupt, but he wasn't stupid. At first he thought if he ignored her—this powerless woman—she would go away. But she did not give up. Every few nights she was back, calling out for the judgment she deserved from him, and waking up the neighbors.

It wasn't long before she became an embarrassment to him. Villagers began to look at him with disgust and anger. They had had enough of his horrible behavior and blatant failure to do his job.

Finally the nocturnal shouting stopped. One morning I said to my mother, "Rafca hasn't woken us up for a week. Did she give up?" I was teasing my mother with this question. I knew what had happened but I wanted to hear her version of the story. My mother's eyes flashed at me in surprise. Sometimes she didn't know when I was leading her on. She asked, "Didn't I tell you that Rafca prayed every day to Yahweh and that she would not give up until her prayers were answered?" This time my teasing backfired on me. I regretted my remark and agreed that I had indeed remembered her faith and determination.

"She got from that judge what was rightly hers from the start. He respected neither God nor man, but Rafca kept praying and never lost heart."

Then it hit me, how God comes through for us in the most ordinary ways and for our daily needs; even through bad people and circumstances God's mercy and justice are manifested.

I began to ponder how I might use this experience to someday teach others about the necessity of praying always and never losing heart.

I will tell them the story of the widow and the rotten judge, I decided. I knew they'd get it.

AUNT HANNAH: HIS MOTHER'S SISTER

Near the cross of Jesus there stood his mother, his mother's sister, Mary the wife of Clopas, and Mary Magdalene. John 19:25

I could see in Aunt Hannah and my mother the unique love between sisters. I used to watch them with fascination when they were together. It is difficult to put into words the magical spark that sisters share. When I was a child I took for granted the visits of my Aunt Hannah and my Uncle Zachary. They came to see us in Nazareth, or we visited with them at my grandparents' home after our journeys to Jerusalem for important religious feasts. My mother and her sister would start talking with such concentration that the rest of us felt like observant strangers of someone else's experience. My grandmother would call them both to the kitchen for help with the food. Off they'd go, still chatting in the language of women who know exactly what to say, and who are unwilling to let anything disrupt the flow of words.

Like most children, I did not begin to value the gift of aunts and uncles until I was an adult in my 20s. Families take each person and their role for granted until the day they realize how lucky they are to have them in their lives. I was no exception.

Among my mother, my grandmother, my aunt, and their cousin Elizabeth, I was nurtured and mentored in the mysteries of women. They who taught me to respect and appreciate the important—but undervalued—role of women in the family, the community, and society. And the ways they fawned over me weren't hard to take, either. I'll admit it, they spoiled me with attentiveness and fierce loyalty. My mother was not a hard disciplinarian, but when my Aunt Hannah was around I saw her eyes flash and her brows scrunch when my mother corrected me. I'll also admit I knew how

27

to make the best of every situation when Aunt Hannah visited. I could do no wrong in her eyes. I loved it!

Aunt Hannah was anxious for me to marry and to enlarge our family. I'm sure she and my mother shared their thoughts about this subject. My mother was more intuitive about my calling in life, but neither of them was prepared for the day they watched me die on a cross as a criminal. What mother could ever be prepared for such a day? My mother and Aunt Hannah were there with the wife of Clopas and Mary Magdalene.

There is no way my mother could have endured the agony of my crucifixion without her sister by her side. Both were in shock at the horror of it all, but they stayed near me as they clung to each other, as sisters do. If there was one thing to be grateful for on that sad, agonizing day, it was Aunt Hannah's support of my terrified, helpless mother. She could not have endured to see my horrifying death if her sister had not been there.

In flesh and in spirit, these two sisters were gifts to me as much as they were to each other.

DANCING GIRL: Abused and Damaged

*On one occasion Herod the tetrarch, having heard of Jesus'
reputation, exclaimed to his courtiers, "This man is John the
Baptizer—it is he in person, raised from the dead; that is why such
miraculous powers are at work in him!" Recall that Herod had
had John arrested, put in chains, and imprisoned on account of
Herodias, the wife of his brother Philip. That was because John
had told him, "It is not right for you to live with her." Herod [and
Herodias Mark 6:19] wanted to kill John but [were] afraid of the
people, who regarded him as a prophet.*

*Then on Herod's birthday Herodias' daughter performed a dance
before the court which delighted Herod so much that he swore he
would grant her anything she asked for. [She...said to her mother,
"What shall I ask for?" Mark. 6:24] Prompted by her mother she
said, "Bring me the head of John the Baptizer on a platter." The
king immediately had his misgivings, but because of his oath and
the guests who were present he gave orders that the request be
granted. He sent the order to have John beheaded in prison.
John's head was brought in on a platter and given to the girl, who
took it to her mother.*

*Later his disciples presented themselves to carry his body away
and bury it. Afterward, they came and informed Jesus. Matthew
14:1-12*

I could see her in my imagination, the eyes of a damaged child.
Her mother's vindictiveness and her uncle's cowardice had put her
in the middle of their evil desires and made her the victim.

When the disciples of John came to me and told me he had been decapitated on the order of Herod, the Roman king of the nation occupying our land, my heart sank. My beloved cousin, my childhood playmate and my forerunner was dead, and for so petty a reason.

Herod had John arrested after calling out the king for having an affair with his sister-in-law Herodias. Herod and Herodias both wanted John to be silenced and to disappear for embarrassing them. Herod could have given the order of execution immediately but he knew John had many followers and was afraid of bringing even more attention to himself and his lover. I knew John had been arrested, but I thought Herod's fear of the people would keep John alive.

It was not so much Herod I worried about, but Herodias. She was determined to see John dead for his brazen outspokenness and for publicly humiliating her, a high-ranking politician's wife. She waited for her chance and pounced when she saw her opening.

What I heard from John's followers was that her daughter danced magnificently at the birthday party Herod threw for his court circle, military officers, and the leading men of Galilee. More than one hundred guests at the celebration were magnetized by her grace and the way her young body moved perfectly in tune with the music. Her veils and dress and shoes sparkled in the light and were reflected in the eyes of the guests.

Herod was so delighted that, drunk with wine and his own power, he promised to give her anything she wanted, to show his appreciation.

The girl was gleeful. Her mind began a long list of things a dancer loves: beautiful shoes, silken scarves, skirts that fly out and up when the body twirls. She couldn't decide which she should request, so she asked for her mother's input. I could imagine her skipping to her mother to help her choose from so many wonderful options. "What should I ask for, mother?"

Herodias smiled with the evil victory of the predator that has captured the long-sought prey. Herod had given his word and the unsuspecting daughter had stepped into a trap. Herodias whispered to her daughter to ask for the head of John the Baptizer on a plate.

The dancing maiden leapt backward from her mother as from a burning veil. "That is not what I want," she declared. "That is your desire!" Herodias persisted, "It is a prize worthy of such a wonderful dance. Tell your uncle your decision."

When John's friends told me this, my head and shoulders caved in defeat, the same way the dancer's whole body must have reacted when she turned to Herod to give him her decision. Only a minute earlier she imagined new shoes and hair jewels. Now, in a monotone voice of defeat she repeated her mother's command, "Give me the head of John the Baptizer on a plate."

That was the one request Herod was not prepared to hear or to grant, but he had given his word and was willing to murder someone rather than appear weak or embarrass himself. Herodias sat back with a satisfied smirk and glowering eyes. Revenge and hatred and self-righteousness had won the day.

My narrators continued with the horrible details. Shocked silence overcame the party as all eyes followed the soldier who walked across the dance floor and handed the girl a bloody, gruesome platter which contained a human head, grisly and still steaming in the cool evening air. The young girl took the heavy platter without the smallest emotional reaction. She struggled to walk steadily toward the table of honor where her mother and uncle sat and dropped it down hard between them. Blood and tissue splattered on

31

everyone nearby. John's open eyes stared at Herod, who jumped up and ran from the room, terrified. I knew Herod would be haunted by those eyes whenever he closed his own.

Herodias, still smiling triumphantly, began to methodically dab John's blood from her face and arms, careful not to smudge her makeup. Her daughter looked into her eyes then turned and walked out of the room and out of her mother's life, never again to become the pawn of evil.

When the disciples of John finished, I wanted to go to her and tell her she would heal and that her experience could eventually help her to be a strong and wise woman who could do much good in the world. But I myself was suffering wrenching grief. I dreaded having to tell my mother our John was dead.

I wept for John the Baptizer and for the dancing girl who only wanted new shoes.

DAUGHTER OF JAIRUS: GRATEFUL PARENTS

Now when Jesus had crossed back to the other side again in the boat, a large crowd gathered around him and he stayed close to the lake. One of the officials of the synagogue, a man named Jairus, came near. Seeing Jesus, he fell at his feet and made this earnest appeal: "My little daughter is critically ill. Please come and lay your hands on her so that she may get well and live." The two went off together and a large crowd followed, pushing against Jesus…. people from the official's house arrived saying, "Your daughter is dead. Why bother the Teacher further?" Jesus disregarded the report that had been brought and said to the official: "Fear is useless. What is needed is trust." He would not permit anyone to follow him except Peter, James, and James' brother John. As they approached the house of the synagogue leader, Jesus was struck by the noise of people wailing and crying loudly on all sides. He entered and said to them: "Why do you make this din with your wailing? The child is not dead. She is asleep." At this they began to ridicule him. Then he put them all out. Jesus took the child's father and mother and his own companions and entered the room where the child lay. Taking her hand, he said to her, "Talitha, koum," which means, "Little girl, get up." The girl, a child of twelve, stood up immediately and began to walk around. At this the family's astonishment knew no bounds. He enjoined them strictly not to let anyone know about it, and told them to give her something to eat. Mark 5:21-24; 35-43

I could see in her the calm trust of a daughter who adored her father, even as she lay completely still on the bed. She had the same color hair as her father, Jairus, the synagogue official. When

33

he approached me and asked me to come to his home to heal his little girl, I knew the situation was dire. There was no way I could refuse the plea of a father whose whole world revolved around his daughter and was, at that moment, crashing.

He asked me if I would lay my hands on her so that she would be healthy again. I was surprised that a synagogue leader had so much faith in me, but he was an exception. He had the true faith that I wished for every Jew. How could I refuse one of God's Chosen who believed in me?

We were close to the house when relatives of Jairus approached to tell us that the child had died, so there was no need for me now. Jairus fell to his knees and sobbed. I suggested we keep going to the house. Inside were dozens of friends and relatives weeping and groaning from the depths of their grief. It was chaotic. I asked what was wrong and they said she had just died, that I was too late. "No," I said. "She's not dead, she's sleeping." I had already healed her at that moment.

Those in the house became angry with me, thinking me stupid and arrogant. So I told everyone to leave the room except the parents and Peter, James, and John. We all stood around the bed. She looked like an angel lying there, so pure and peaceful. Her hands were folded on her chest. The only sound was the choked sobs of her mother and father, who held each other for strength.

They could not see her chest moving as she breathed. Nor did they notice the color returning to her cheeks as we stood there. Now it was time for her to wake up and ask her mother and father why they were crying.

I lifted one of her small, delicate hands from her chest and placed it in both of mine. It was cool, no more fever. I didn't know her name, so I said, "Little girl, get up now." Her eyes opened immediately and her parents gasped. She sat up and smiled at them. I could she see had her mother's hazel-brown eyes. She put her feet on the floor and stood up. Her parents' joy was beyond description. They flew to her and surrounded her with their arms and bodies. "Mommy, daddy, why are you crying?" she asked.

Their daughter was still weak from her illness and needed to gain her strength back before she could return to her school and friends. So I said, "Give her something to eat." Her body had been through a lot, but she was on the mend. The worst was over.

ELIZABETH AND MARY: COUSINS

Afterward, his [Zachariah's] wife Elizabeth conceived. She went into seclusion for five months, saying: "In these days the Lord is acting on my behalf; he has seen fit to remove my reproach among men."...Thereupon Mary set out, proceeding in haste into the hill country to a town of Judah, where she entered Zechariah's house and greeted Elizabeth. When Elizabeth heard Mary's greeting, the baby leapt in her womb. Elizabeth was filled with the Holy Spirit and cried out in a loud voice: "Blest are you among women and blest is the fruit of your womb. But who am I that the mother of my Lord should come to me? The moment your greeting sounded in my ears, the baby leapt in my womb for joy. Blest is she who trusted that the Lord's words to her would be fulfilled." Luke 1:24; 39-45

I could see in the animated eyes of my mother the same excitement she must have felt thirty-one years earlier when the angel told her that her older cousin, Elizabeth, was six months pregnant. My mother was a young girl at the time, newly betrothed to my father. Her life had been normal, common, and uneventful until that day when God's angel showed up and changed everything permanently.

In spite of the fact that I was an adult when I asked her to tell me once again the story of the angel, my eyes were magnetized to my mother as she presented the facts of my conception and birth. It really was a gift that she confided in me what happened to her and her cousin so many years ago. I was amazed and profoundly impressed by what God had brought forth through these two women: one who was barely a woman, and the other who was beyond the age nature intends for childbirth.

My mother kept the story to herself for the first twenty-five years of my life. There was no reason for her to share it with me until then, when my cousin John began preaching and baptizing.

John was the son of Elizabeth and Zachariah. He was six months older than I. We played together as children when our family visited them in the hill country of Judea, or when Elizabeth and John came down to Nazareth to visit us after Zachariah died.

John was a teenager when his mother died. There was talk of his coming to live with us, my mother told me, but John had been independent and headstrong since the day he was born and refused to live with anyone. He cared for himself, and it was obvious after a while that he had no family life where he was fed and clothed properly. Through the years we heard stories of John, clothed with the skins of animals and eating wild honey and locusts. I cringed when I heard that. *Locusts?* I thought. *No thanks.* John was marching to the beat of his own drummer, serving Yahweh way outside the box of our religious customs. That was John.

Many times I asked my mother to tell me again the story of the angel. She would look at me with eyes that asked, *My son, how old are you? You are well beyond the age when children want a story repeated again and again.* But when she saw my smile and my total attention, she was once more transported back to that amazing time in her life.

She always began with, "I was just a maiden..." That's when her eyes would light up and I could see her return in her imagination to a time and place she had revisited a thousand times already. "I actually saw an angel," she said with the same amazed reaction she must have had the day it happened. Her whole body seemed to glow with the wonder of it. "And the angel told me my older cousin, Elizabeth, was pregnant! It was miraculous! Elizabeth had long ago resigned herself to being childless. She loved me as a daughter. My mother took me often to visit her so that Elizabeth could fuss over me like a mother and be blessed with the love I showed her. When I became a woman and my father betrothed me to your father, I was much too young to comprehend the life consequences of that custom, but there was nothing I could do about it anyway. It is our way. And then that angel showed up in my bedroom and told me I was going to have a baby and so was Elizabeth!

"I was speechless with amazement and joy. I told my mother I needed to see Elizabeth right away. When I told her Elizabeth was pregnant, my mother put her hand on my forehead to check for fever. She wondered where I had come up with such a tale. Of course she didn't want me to go on the journey but I was already packing."

I sat there with my chin in my hand and my elbow propped on the bread table. My favorite part of the story was coming up.

"When I got to her house I ran through the door shouting, 'Elizabeth, where are you?! It's Mary – I'm here for you!' My cousin appeared from around the corner and held out her arms in joy. I saw the bulge in her dress and ran to embrace her and the one she carried within.

"What a day that was," my mother sighed, moving her head from side to side, still lost in the wonder of the memory. Then she said, "I am now close to the age Elizabeth was when she gave birth to John. I can't imagine having a baby now," she confessed, "But Elizabeth was never too old for anything God called her to do. She was amazing. She taught me so much about faith in Yahweh. I miss her still."

And then my mother's eyes would tear up. I'd wrap my arms around her and kiss the top of her head. I loved that story.

FRIENDS FAITHFUL: WATCH AND WAIT

A great crowd of people followed him, including women who beat their breasts and lamented over him...all his friends and the women who had accompanied him from Galilee were standing at a distance watching everything...the women who had come with him from Galilee followed along behind. They saw the tomb and how his body was buried. Luke 23:27,49,55

I could see them all along the way as I slowly walked the hill to my death. They were crying. They did not understand how this could be happening to me. But they did not know the dark side of politics or mob rule or even jealousy. What they knew was goodness and mercy and the important things about life, like family love and forgiveness and friendship. It was the power of their gratitude that enabled them to walk with me on my death walk.

They struggled through a wall of people on either side of me as I took each painful step. These women from Galilee, who had supported me and put up with my disciples, were with me to the end. Even now, as they edged their way through this angry, bloodthirsty pack, they did not take their eyes off me.

Not once did they consider going home because it was too painful to watch, and too dangerous to be recognized as my friends. They knew what was going to happen as well as I did. Yet, I continued to see them from the corners of my bloody eyes.

If it weren't for them, I think I would have lost the will to live. But the women did not betray me. They were fearless and determined. Oh, these women! Oh, these friends who never lost faith! They so understood how to deal with life's bad times. And this was, indeed, a very bad time.

But they stayed with me.

They remained on the outer fringe of the crowd that was cheering as I bled to death. Just knowing they were nearby helped me endure those final moments until my body said *'no more.'* I knew they would not leave me, even after my life ended and there was nothing left to do except bury me.

It was going to be a long, sad Sabbath for my friends. My physical pain was not nearly as overwhelming as the heartfelt pain I endured because of what I had caused them to suffer as they watched me die. It was all because of me that they were so defeated, so crushed, and so abandoned.

And still they would be faithful, these strong, capable women of mine. They would wait and watch. They would stay in the background and take note of the cave where my body would be placed until they could bury me. And after the Sabbath ended they would come back with their spices and perfumes and tend to me one last time.

Or so they thought.

GIRL AT THE GATE: PETER IS CALLED OUT

"Lord," [Peter] said to him, "at your side I am prepared to face imprisonment and death itself." Jesus replied, "I tell you, Peter, the cock will not crow today until you have three times denied that you know me."

They led him away under arrest and brought him to the house of the high priest, while Peter followed at a distance. Later they lighted a fire in the middle of the courtyard and were sitting beside it, and Peter sat among them. A servant girl saw him sitting in the light of the fire. She gazed at him intently, then said, "This man was with him." He denied it, saying, "Woman, I do not know him." Luke 22:33-34; 54-57

I could see in her the spunk of the young who don't want societal expectations holding them back. She had just enough common sense and gumption to challenge the rules but not break them. She certainly did not fit in with the role of a woman at that time. But she didn't care. That's what I loved about her: an outspoken honesty that did not fear risk.

On the night before I was killed, when I warned Peter that he was going to deny me—not once, but three times—I knew she would be his first denial. She was a friend of the High Priest's daughter and worked for the family. She and her friends were well aware of my reputation and fame. I knew she would be there to open the gate to the courtyard that night, that terrible night.

When I was inside being interrogated by the ecclesiastical authorities, the leaders who wanted me dead and got their way the next day, Peter was outside trying to stay warm as he waited nervously to learn my fate. At that point, anyone connected with me was in danger of being arrested. It was guilt by association. Peter thought he wouldn't be recognized out there in the dark by the fire, but the servant girl knew him from the many times she had seen us together in the temple and in the town.

As she watched Peter she saw he was trying to blend in and remain undetected. He was acting like someone who was trying to hide, not like the confident right-hand man of Jesus, who was so popular. She stared at him, trying to determine if she was correct. She doubted herself because Peter looked so worried and fearful. Neither was he joining in the conversation around the fire, saying nothing in defense of his friend Jesus whose fate was being decided at that moment. She wondered what was wrong with him. Did he have no backbone? Was he ashamed to be associated with the one whom he claimed to love?

Yes, she decided, *that's him*. "This man was with him," she stated aloud. She challenged his loyalty and his love for me. She hoped he would meet the challenge and stand up for me, despite the probable negative consequence of doing so.

It's amazing how the simplest of words or situations can be the beginning-of-the-end or the door to abundance. At that moment Peter felt trapped. He could have ignored this bold, young woman who dared to be out after dark and who spoke so confidently. *Who does she think she is?* he thought. He expected to end the discussion with a simple verbal denial. The men surely would take his word over hers. He knew he had the advantage so he said, "Woman, I do not know him," and continued rubbing his cold hands near the fire.

She continued to stare at Peter in silence, seeing right through his hypocrisy and his lie. What a coward, she thought. No spine.

44

But she knew about loyalty to friends and the courage it sometimes took to stand by those you love, no matter the personal price you paid in doing so. She knew I was worth defending. She never would have denied me. I knew it. This servant girl at the gate had the strength of character I wanted in a follower. I was sure that someday women such as this one would fearlessly speak out for me despite the risk, unlike my friend Peter, who just then heard the cock crow.

HER PERFUME: FOREVER REMEMBERED

While Jesus was in Bethany at the house of Simon the leper, a woman carrying a jar of costly perfume came up to him at table and began to pour it on his head. When the disciples saw this they grew indignant, protesting, "What is the point of such extravagance? This could have been sold for a good price and the money given to the poor." Jesus became aware of this and said to them: "Why do you criticize the woman? It is a good deed she has done for me. The poor you will always have with you but you will not always have me. By pouring this perfume on my body, she has contributed toward my burial preparation. I assure you, wherever the good news is proclaimed throughout the world, what she did will be spoken of as her memorial. Matthew 26:6-13

I could see in her the need to express her love without words. She didn't have to say anything; what she did said it all. She gave up a lot to purchase that expensive oil. It smelled so good. I could see the joy in her eyes and I felt the love in her fingers as she spread the oil on my head, and then my feet. Without a word she touched me and I felt her intense energy. It was the vibration of gratitude and absolute appreciation for my presence.

She had thought to herself, quite rightly, *He will know what I am trying to express. I won't need to say anything. He will know why I am there and will allow me to honor Him with expensive oil on His skin. I have not lust for Him. What I feel in my heart is far beyond physical need or union. No. My soul has been touched and caressed by this man's wisdom. His eyes have penetrated that part of me that no man's body can enter. He has seen the depths of me and loved me there. This oil is symbolic. He knows who I am! And I know, too, because of him. No words are needed between us.*

I knew her thoughts and I let her touch me with the expensive, sweet-smelling oil. It felt so good on my skin. My disciples, in their usual thickheaded manner, didn't have a clue what was happening. They began calculating cost and exchanging money for potential services. Were they saying I didn't deserve such treatment? Did they believe I was not worthy to be anointed?

As usual, I had to bring the sublime down to a level they could relate to. I told them she was anointing my body for burial. They understood that concept even if they didn't get the message that soon I would die. And then I told them, "She will be forever remembered for this beautiful gesture." They didn't get that, either, but it didn't bother me.

And then I smiled because I knew that this silent, generous friend would have a permanent place in my story. And she deserves it.

HERODIAS: ANTI-WOMAN

Recall that Herod had had John arrested, put in chains, and imprisoned on account of Herodias, the wife of his brother Philip....Then on Herod's birthday Herodias' daughter performed a dance before the court which delighted Herod so much that he swore he would grant her anything she asked for. Prompted by her mother she said, "Bring me the head of John the Baptizer on a platter." ...John's head was brought in on a platter and given to the girl, who took it to her mother. Matthew 14:3-4, 6-8, 11.

I could see in Herodias a ruthless ambition, refined manipulation, and granite-like ego. Nowhere in her aura could I pick up the energy of love, compassion, or peace. I felt a chill when she came to my mind. Herodias presented an outward beauty that masked an inward ugliness that leaked out and stained everything and everyone around her. All the creams and potions in the world could not conceal the cold heart that was revealed in her dark, merciless eyes.

She had a way with men. Herodias knew their cravings and how to satisfy their lusts. The expert manipulator, she used men to work her way up the social ladder to become the king's lover, who also was her brother-in-law. At last she had reached the top as the politician's wife who was to be condescended to, or suffer her vengeance.

Her influential power murdered John the Baptist, my forerunner, which meant I would soon follow—once again—in his footsteps. I was not afraid of her. The shiver I felt came from the shock of evil energy that chilled the air she breathed.

Only one of us could survive her need for control, conquest, and self-aggrandizement. It would not be me.

HIS MARYS: MORNING HAS BROKEN

After the Sabbath, as the first day of the week was dawning, Mary Magdalene came with the other Mary to inspect the tomb. Suddenly there was a mighty earthquake as the angel of the Lord descended from heaven. He came to the stone, rolled it back, and sat on it. In appearance he resembled a flash of lightning while his garments were as dazzling as snow. The guards grew paralyzed with fear of him and fell down like dead men. The angel spoke, addressing the women: "Do not be frightened. I know you are looking for Jesus the crucified, but he is not here. He has been raised, exactly as he promised. Come and see the place where he was laid. Then go quickly and tell the disciples: 'He has been raised from the dead and now goes ahead of you to Galilee, where you will see him.' That is the message I have for you." They hurried away from the tomb half-overjoyed, half-fearful, and ran to carry the good news to his disciples. Suddenly, without warning, Jesus stood before them and said, "Peace!" The women came up and embraced his feet and did him homage. Matthew 28: 1-9

I could see in them an equal measure of excitement and fear. The angel had nearly scared them to death with its brilliance and its message, "He is not here." They had come in grief to clean and anoint my lifeless body with oil, and here they were, on their way to tell my disciples that I had been raised from the dead and planned to meet them in Galilee.

They were running down the path, away from the huge boulder that had been rolled in front of the entrance to my grave. Until the moment of shock when they saw the angel and an empty tomb, their biggest concern had been not knowing how they were going to move the massive rock aside to get to me. Now here they come, running, not quite sure how to feel or what to believe. They knew

51

for sure I was not in the tomb anymore, but *alive*? Yet, who could doubt an angel of the Lord?

I was overjoyed to see them again, my Marys, these tremendous friends who stood by me, even under the bloody, horrifying cross of my execution. What can be said about this kind of love, this loyalty? I couldn't wait to speak with them, to be near them, to thank them for never letting me down.

I knew the disciples would not believe it when the women told them they had seen an angel who actually spoke to them. Neither would they believe I had come back to life. Who would believe such a message, especially from women. But these were not ordinary women. They were *my* women, *my* magnificent friends. I could no longer hold back my excitement. As they came down the hill I stepped into the path and stood there facing them. They saw me but did not recognize me. I raised my hand and waved to them as I always used to. With a smile I said, "Peace!"

Both Marys froze in place, shocked to silence. Who would not be stunned to see standing before you (smiling, no less) the one you watched die an agonizing death just two days earlier. Their eyes were still red from endless tears as they stood in shocked disbelief, staring at me. Nothing came out of their mouths, but quickly the tears started to flow once more, this time in joy; in utter, unbelievable happiness.

Soon enough they found their legs and flew to me. They fell to the ground and began kissing the feet of their Lord, these same feet that had been so recently crusted with blood and hammered with rusty spikes.

But that was then. And this is now, together again. ALIVE!

JOANNA: Glad to Help

After this he journeyed through towns and villages preaching and proclaiming the good news of the kingdom of God. The Twelve accompanied him, and also some women who had been cured of evil spirits and maladies; Mary called the Magdalene, from whom seven devils had gone out, Joanna, the wife of Herod's steward Chuza, Susanna, and many others who were assisting them out of their means. Luke 8:1-3

I could see in Joanna a sad emptiness that not even the luxury of Herod's home could fill. She was the wife of Chuza, Herod's steward, who was highly respected in the King's palace. Chuza was, after all, in charge of the food and wine in the palace. That alone meant he was a competent planner and manager. Chuza was a busy man, out the door early and home late. His wife, Joanna, did not need to busy herself with the typical tasks of homemaking because of her social status in the palatial world of King Herod. She had time to socialize with other women of the Roman occupation, such as with Pilate's wife, who was a psychic.

Joanna never would have heard of me if it were not for Pilate's wife. The wives of the Roman politicians met with her weekly to hear her predictions and the messages she received from a world unseen. It was Pilate's wife who first mentioned me to the weekly women's group. Joanna was amazed by the dreams and intuitions Pilate's wife shared with the group about me. None of the women could figure out why I was so frequently in the psychic's dreams. Joanna found herself wanting to see me in person, attracted by some inner spark that became an intense yearning whenever my name was mentioned, which was often.

Pilate's wife also wanted to meet the man who so often occupied her subconscious mind in sleep. But she was more restricted than

Joanna in her freedom to walk the city streets and country roads where I might be found. So it was Joanna who gladly volunteered to check out the miracle worker whom multitudes were following and who was causing a fuss among the Jewish hierarchy.

The first time I saw Joanna in the crowd I knew who she was. Her heart jumped when our eyes met. She felt her soul fill up, no longer empty or sad. From that day on I saw her frequently in the crowds that surrounded my disciples and me. She became one of the women who provided provisions for us every day. Her husband, Chuza, was delighted by the new spark of life he saw in his wife. She no longer suffered the depressive episodes that confined her to her room for weeks at a time. He gladly gave her the supplies and food she asked for, no questions asked.

Pilate's wife continued to see me in her dreams. She also dreamt of Joanna. She had seen a darkness enveloping Joanna, but there remained within her friend a glowing flame that the darkness could not extinguish. She interpreted these symbols as the forces of good and evil in the soul of her friend. She said the flame of love in Joanna would never permit her dark depression to ever again touch her. That protective, healing fire is the gift of my love to this beautiful friend. She is safe.

JUDITH: Her Life is Saved

At daybreak he reappeared in the temple area; and when the people started coming to him, he sat down and began to teach them. The scribes and the Pharisees led a woman forward who had been caught in adultery. They made her stand there in front of everyone.

"Teacher," they said to him, "this woman has been caught in the act of adultery. In the law, Moses ordered such women to be stoned. What do you have to say about the case?"

(They were posing this question to trap him, so that they could have something to accuse him of.)

Jesus bent down and started tracing on the ground with his finger. When they persisted in their questioning, he straightened up and said to them, "Let the man among you who has no sin be the first to cast a stone at her." A second time he bent down and wrote on the ground.

Then the audience drifted away one by one, beginning with the elders. This left him alone with the woman, who continued to stand there before him. Jesus finally straightened up and said to her, "Woman, where did they all disappear to? Has no one condemned you?" "No one, sir," she answered. Jesus said, "Nor do I condemn you." John 8:2-10

I could see her embarrassment and defeat. I watched her accusers dragging her into the temple like a worthless, broken jar about to be smashed to pieces and tossed in a garbage heap. She kept tripping because her legs couldn't keep up with the pace of these merciless religious leaders who were supposed to love the Law of

Moses. Instead, they were about to use the law for their own benefit and her execution.

These were not real men who cared about my people; they didn't value this woman any more than they valued the law of God. They used the law to get their way. I knew they would soon trap me, too, by twisting and stretching the law to their own advantage, just as they were about to do to her. She and I had this in common: they were out to get us and they would use God's written word to justify murder.

She stood in front of me looking at the ground as the scribes and Pharisees gleefully displayed their sinner and laid out their fail-proof case for the death penalty. They knew I couldn't dispute what Moses said about what should be done with women caught in adultery. *What about the **man** caught in adultery?* I wondered. Why was Moses silent about the adulterous partner?

She still had not looked up at me. I wanted to look into her eyes and give her some sign of compassion, of redemption. But she stood there, head bent. So I stooped down and started writing in the sand in the direct line of her vision. I wrote her name, Judith. Her eyes widened, but she did not look up. She wondered how I knew her. How could I not know her?

Then I stood up. They really thought they had me. I couldn't deny what Moses wrote and yet these scholars knew me well enough to realize I would never bless a ruthless death by stoning. At least they knew that much about me. The scribes were not stupid. They knew the issue was punishment for sin. Sin offends my Father. Moses did not go easy on those who offended God.

And that's when I did a little law-twisting of my own. Without judging Judith, I agreed with Moses' demand that sinners be punished before I invited the sinless in the group to step forward and begin the stoning. Only those without sin have the right to condemn sinners. Only the sinless deserve no punishment.

Judith began to tremble and weep so I bent down quickly and wrote "forgiven" in the sand below her eyes. It was only then that she looked at my face. I could see in her a mix of gratitude and relief. If only Moses had known the power of forgiveness. But Moses was dealing with the same type of hateful, self-righteous sinners that had dragged Judith from her bedroom trap to me.

When I stood up again only the two of us were there. The ground around us was littered with fist-sized rocks intended for Judith's death.

"Where did everyone go?" I asked her. "Isn't anyone left to condemn you?"

"No, Sir," she responded, not knowing what I would do to her or what I might want in return for saving her.

"Then I won't, either." I said.

She looked at me then. She could see in me a man very different from the one she was caught with and the ones who condemned her. She knew I was not out for my own satisfaction. In me she saw respect and appreciation and wonder. Isn't that what every woman wants?

LOT'S WIFE: NO GOING BACK

As dawn was breaking the angels urged Lot on saying, "On your way! Take with you your wife and your two daughters who are here, or you will be swept away in the punishment of the city."...But Lot's wife looked back, and she was turned into a pillar of salt. Genesis 19:15,26

"Remember Lot's wife. Whoever tries to preserve his life will lose it; whoever loses it will keep it." Luke 17:32-33

I could see in Lot's wife the dilemma of one who cannot let go and move on. She embodied the outcome of refusing to release the people, places, and things that were destroying her.

I felt sorry for Lot's wife. She was only human, after all. She loved her lifestyle in Sodom. She didn't want anything to change. She didn't understand that life requires change; life *is* change. Nothing stays the same.

Lot's wife had it all. She was blessed with a good husband and two beautiful daughters. She wanted to maintain the status quo. Her motto was, "Protect and preserve what we have." She didn't believe there were no guarantees in life. Lot's wife thought she could control her world, preserve it, salt it, so nothing went bad.

But bad things happen to good people.

When I reminded them of Lot's wife, what I wanted to teach my followers was that you can't prevent damage and injustice in this imperfect world. A life can be torn to shreds in a moment, or overnight, as I would find out shortly myself.

I understood where Lot's wife was coming from in her reluctance and resentment. But what she lacked—and this is why I pitied her—was trust in the angels' guidance to safety and salvation. Instead, she wanted to go back to what she had before the angels told her it was time to leave or be destroyed.

There's no going back. You must let go and trust the angels to guide you forward.

MARTHA: Chief Cook & CEO

On their journey Jesus entered a village where a woman named Martha welcomed him to her home. She had a sister named Mary, who seated herself at the Lord's feet and listened to his words. Martha, who was busy with all the details of hospitality, came to him and said, "Lord, are you not concerned that my sister has left me to do the household tasks all alone? Tell her to help me."

The Lord in reply said to her: "Martha, Martha, you are anxious and upset about many things; one thing only is required. Mary has chosen the better portion and she shall not be deprived of it." Luke 10:38-42

I could see in Martha a leader. In another age she would have become the head of a nation. But in this age, because she is a woman in a no-name village without personal or political or religious power, the full expression of her innate ability would never be manifest. Yet, in her own way she was able to use her talents in the everyday tasks of life.

And she owned her own home. I smiled when Peter told me she had invited the crowd of us to dinner in her home. "*Her* home?" I asked. "Yes, Lord," Peter responded. "Apparently she has her own income through a business she runs, and she inherited a home for herself and her sister." *This is a woman I want to meet*, I said to myself. It didn't take much imagination to start listing the obstacles this woman encountered on her way to business and home ownership. I knew I was in for a treat.

"Tell her we'll come for dinner," I said to a surprised Peter. After all this time as my right-hand man, Peter still couldn't predict when I would respond to an invitation. But he should have figured out by now that my choices always are outside the boundaries of predictable. I am as attracted to strong, smart women as I am to little children and to those who suffer.

Her name was Martha. She possessed every bit of competency I expected. I knew right away that her business must have something to do with food because she was totally in control of the accoutrements of hospitality and food preparation. Even though she was giving orders to helpers right and left, she was in total control of the chaos. It's no easy feat to host my disciples and me when we blow through town without much warning. My presence draws a crowd. Before you know it, everyone is hungry. Martha was in for a challenge and she knew it as soon as we hit her doorstep.

She and her sister, Mary, were delightful hostesses. Martha was thrilled to have us in her space, to make us feel at home, and to share with us her culinary talents. Her home was large. I supposed she rented rooms for events and catered them as well.

Martha couldn't spare much time to talk, so she told Mary to help us relax and wash up for the meal. After that she was to return to the kitchen. Mary was Martha's opposite: calm, undisturbed, relaxed, and untroubled. Nothing bothered Mary. She was not one to fret over the details of table settings or the timing of baking bread. Mary simply cared about the comfort of her guests. She attended to their needs in the present moment without worrying about anything else.

Most of the time the differences between the two balanced themselves out. But today was not a typical meal where friends gather. A couple dozen men, dirty and hungry, had just come through the door. As we took turns washing up, Mary asked me about my preaching and the tales of cures that had people buzzing.

She looked at me with curiosity, but also with eyes of faith in the power of love to heal.

As Mary and I spoke and I told her about my mission and the love of God, I could see Martha in the background, glaring out at us from the kitchen every few minutes with a look of growing frustration. She could see that Mary was seated at my feet with her arms wrapped around her folded legs. Mary was lost in the moment, as usual, soaking in my words and my presence.

A couple of times Martha caught my eye and gestured at Mary. She was giving me a signal to tell Mary to come help her in the kitchen. I ignored her. I knew she could handle everything without Mary, and I was enjoying these moments with her sister. As the time approached to serve her wonderful meal, Martha's frustration got the best of her. She stomped out of the kitchen toward her sister, sitting there as calm as could be. I think Martha was more annoyed with me than with Mary because she knew I did not tell Mary to go help her with the meal preparations.

Martha, the manager, the leader, was not used to being ignored. She knew that I knew she was asking me to get Mary up and into the kitchen where she was needed. But I, too, love the present moment when I can open my heart to a sincere listener and I didn't want to be deprived of this pleasure.

Martha, annoyed, asked me, "Lord, don't you care that Mary has burdened me with her duties in the kitchen? I need her to get up and help me **now**. Please tell her to give me a hand." That's what I loved about Martha, her honest and practical evaluation of the situation. No wonder she had so many good workers around her. She was fair. And in this moment she was right, of course. But the meal would be delicious even if Mary was slacking.

I wanted to tell Martha I didn't love her less than Mary because she was in the kitchen and Mary was here talking to me without a care in the world. But Martha couldn't see that life's smallest pleasures and treasures are about choices we make. Martha knew as well as I did that with or without Mary in the kitchen the meal would be perfect. But her expectations were frustrated by Mary's choice, and the manager in her was upset.

I had to smile at Martha, standing over me with sweat on her cheeks, ladle in hand, and frown on brow. Hers was the frustration of every cook who needed an extra pair of hands, but no volunteers. Martha was in her element and she wanted Mary there with her. But Mary's was a different element, a different calling. Martha's choice was satisfying to her extrovert spirit, just as Mary's calling satisfied her inner being. Martha liked the commotion, the challenge of balancing many balls in the air at once. She was a mixture of risk and control and dare.

I wanted Martha to know that Mary's choice to relax with me for a while was giving me as much pleasure as I knew her meal would be giving me, very soon. But in the moment, Martha only saw that Mary's choice impacted her negatively, and I was a contributor to her current annoyed state.

The best I could do was to put the situation in the context of choice. Poor Martha. She wouldn't get it, but I told her that Mary had made a choice, a good choice, to sit with me and talk. I wasn't about to tell her to leave me when she was glowing with happiness at my feet and I felt so comforted by her presence. I couldn't take that from her—or me.

MARY MAGDALENE: HIS LOVE

Many women were present looking on from a distance. They had followed Jesus from Galilee to attend to his needs. Among them were Mary Magdalene, and Mary the mother of James and Joseph, and the mother of Zebedee's sons. Matthew 27:55-56

Meanwhile, Mary Magdalene and Mary the mother of Joses observed where he had been laid. When the Sabbath was over, Mary Magdalene, Mary the mother of James, and Salome bought perfumed oils with which they intended to go and anoint Jesus. Mark 15:47; 16:1

The twelve accompanied him, and also some women who had been cured of evil spirits and maladies; Mary called the Magdalene, from whom seven devils had gone out, Joanna, the wife of Herod's steward Chuza, Susanna, and many others who were assisting them out of their means. Luke 8:1-3

The women were Mary of Magdala, Joanna, and Mary the mother of James. The other women with them also told the apostles... Luke 24:10

Near the cross of Jesus there stood his mother, his mother's sister, Mary the wife of Clopas, and Mary Magdalene. John 19:25

I could see in the Magdalen's eyes the stars of the night sky and the ocean's depths. I could hear in her voice the sounds of angels' wings and gentle breezes. I felt security in her presence and aching abandonment when she was not near me.

There were many Marys in my life and I loved them all, most especially my mother. The mother of James and Joseph was a Mary. The mother of Joses and the mother of the other James both were named Mary, as was the wife of Clopas.

But there was one Mary whom I loved with a love that I had for no other. It was the precious love that a man has for the woman who has stolen his heart. She was the Mary that made my eyes light up when I saw her, and who made my heart jump when I heard her voice.

I loved everything about her. And I knew everything about her, inside-out. She was mine because I loved her soul and because she knew I loved her as no other man ever would. We connected to the best in each other and we complemented each other. I trusted her and wanted her near me.

I'm not sure my mother saw in her what I did, at first. She knew we loved each other; mothers see and know such things. If my mother had any doubts about Mary's intentions or her sincerity, they were dismissed when she stood by my mother's side at my execution. It was Mary of Magdala who watched where they placed my body, and she was there before dawn on the day after the Sabbath to anoint me for burial.

She was the one I wanted to see first. I couldn't wait for that first dawn. Not even death could keep me from her.

Is it any wonder I understood and appreciated God's magnificence in all women? There was just something about my personhood that could draw out the best in them, no matter what their station in life, their age, or their life experience. I admired their intuition, their friendships, and their ruthless power to care for those they loved. They held life together.

Societies would put them down, but they have their ways. They are smarter than the men who try to control them. They suffer tremendously because of men and their lusts, but they never give up! These maidens, these mothers, these wise crones! They are smart and resourceful. They know men better than men know themselves or each other.

That's what I loved about Mary Magdalene. She saw herself in me and I saw myself in her, like two mirrors reflecting the luminous love of the other. We connected and we gave to each other from our individual depths, even as we drew life itself from the other's heart.

Who can describe that love? I know I can't, not in human words. Still, I wish this love for every person who lives, all men and all women. There would be such peace in the world if everyone had the love, trust, and joy that she and I shared and gave to the world.

There was no possessiveness in my love for my followers. That is why so many women looked after me and provided what my disciples and I needed from day to day. Each one loved me and experienced my personal, exclusive love for her. There was no mystery about it. I was happy to give them what they needed in their lives to be appreciated and respected. If only men understood how uncomplicated it is to please a woman!

If men would only look a little closer at the way I treat women and relate to them, they too would attract into their lives the love like that which Mary Magdalene had for me. They would experience what I received from her. Oh, how happy they would be! Most men have no idea of the fulfillment a woman can bring to their lives. The joy I speak of is more than the exquisite pleasure of a woman's body. It is about the experience of heaven in a woman's love, her absolute, fierce loyalty for the man in her life.

A man's mother is his first love. He learns from her what true love is and he goes in search of it for his own life. Lucky is that man who finds it. I found it in Mary of Magdala. I loved her.

MIRACLE OF SIGHT: MIXED BLESSING

The Jews refused to believe that he had really been born blind and had begun to see, until they summoned the parents of this man, who now could see. "Is this your son?" the asked, "And if so, do you attest that he was blind at birth? How do you account for the fact that now he can see?" The parents answered, "We know this is our son, and we know he was blind at birth. But how he can see now, or who opened his eyes, we have no idea. Ask him. He is old enough to speak for himself." (His parents answered in this fashion because they were afraid of the Jews, who had already agreed among themselves that anyone who acknowledged Jesus as the Messiah would be put out of the synagogue. That is why his parents said, "He is of age—ask him.") John 9:18-23

I could see in his mother the speechless amazement of a dream-come-true. Her son, her precious baby boy whose eyes never saw the light of day, had come to her with arms wide when she called his name. She knew since his birth that he would be a blind street beggar all his life. What other option is there for a man who cannot see? Such a person cannot work for others nor support himself. There were no good outcomes for the blind. Still, she and her husband had raised him to take care of himself in spite of his handicap.

And yet I could imagine the mother of this blind young man the day I saw him begging along the road. I could see her influence on him. His mother and father had taught him and trained him to accommodate his fate. I used to see many blind men begging, but I knew this one had a mother whose heart would explode with joy when she looked into the new eyes of her son and he saw her for the first time.

This clever mother recognized the hypocrisy of the religious leaders of our day. She knew their hands were in the pockets of our Roman occupiers. They cared only for their own social status and security, but had no concern for the poor, especially for blind beggars.

She and her husband stood up to the Pharisees who were out to get me. She was not going to be bullied into speaking against the one who had just given sight to her blind child. The Jewish leaders set a trap for this mother and father who were overjoyed by their son's vision and at the same time terrified of the consequences of being expelled from the synagogue.

The parents would not allow the Pharisees to trap them into admitting that I was the Messiah and risk expulsion and its dire consequences. They said, "Our son is an adult. We raised him to speak for himself. Ask him who it was who healed him. He will tell you the truth."

Ah, these are remarkable parents, I thought. *Here is a mother who is as gentle as a dove and as wise as a serpent.* I so loved these mothers who raised their children to speak for themselves and make their way in the world in spite of challenges.

She reminded me of my own mother.

MIRIAM & ELI: BRIDE & GROOM

"On the third day there was a wedding at Cana in Galilee, and the mother of Jesus was there. Jesus and his disciples had likewise been invited to the celebration. At a certain point the wine ran out, and Jesus' mother told him, 'They have no more wine.' Jesus replied, 'Woman, how does this concern of yours involve me? My hour has not yet come.' His mother instructed those waiting on table, 'Do whatever he tells you.' As prescribed for Jewish ceremonial washings, there were at hand six stone water jars, each holding fifteen to twenty-five gallons. 'Fill those jars with water,' Jesus ordered, at which they filled them to the brim." John 2:1-7

I could see that look on my mother's face. She always got to me with that one particular look. Ever since the day twenty years earlier when I pounded the rising bread with my fist and ruined it, my mother had a way of looking at me that moved me to the core and made it impossible to not give her what she wanted. Did all mothers have this power over their sons, I wondered, with a simple look?

She didn't give me "the look" often, but when she did, I knew it was impossible to say no, even if I gave her a hard time, or tried to.

I got the look at Cana during the wedding reception of Eli and Miriam. We all were having a great time dancing, eating, drinking, laughing, and singing. It was a celebration that had been going on for hours and showed no signs of slowing down any time soon. It felt good to relax and not be the center of attention for once. I savored the love between the newlyweds and the joy of their parents.

I would have gone without my disciples, but Miriam's father insisted I bring everyone. At the time he extended the invitation I remember wondering if he even knew how many friends he was talking about when he said, "Bring them all!" My mother was there. I saw her face turn pale but she said nothing.

Eli was my age. He and I studied the Torah together when we were young. He used to tease me about being smarter than the Rabbi. And he was part of the search party that came looking for me the time I decided to stay in Jerusalem without telling my parents. Eli is a merchant now. He will make Miriam happy. It was a good day.

I couldn't hear my mother's words at first, but she had pulled me aside to tell me the wine was all gone. The tone of voice she was using was as though she expected me to do something about it. Like what—go to the village and buy more? I balked. I did not want to do anything to draw attention to myself; not today. I had not yet begun to preach beyond the region and I didn't want to take the focus off Eli and Miriam. So I told my mother the wine supply was not my problem. Wrong answer. She stepped to within six inches of my robe and looked up at me. She gave me the look. Not one word was said between us after that. She just stood there looking into my eyes and straight into my heart until I said, "Okay."

And then she gave me that smile of hers that makes the angels dance. She turned quickly and told the waiters to do whatever I told them to do. I breathed a sigh of relief. She forgave my annoyance. What would be the point of explaining my perspective? She asked so little of me. She was looking out for Eli and Miriam, not herself.

No wine, huh? You want wine? I'll give you wine. "Waiter, fill up those six huge stone jars with water, the ones that hold 25 gallons each. Fill them to the brim." The night was still young.

MOTHER BIRDS: ALL MOTHERS

O Jerusalem, Jerusalem, murderess of prophets and stoner of those who were sent to you! How often have I yearned to gather your children, as a mother bird gathers her young under her wings... Matthew 23:37

I could see in the mother sparrow a calm yet self-assured competence, as she tended her nest. I loved watching mother birds of every kind. They were magnificent in their capacity to breed and brood, feed and care. All mother animals are protective and efficient, but mother birds are special. Maybe it's because we can observe their patterns easier than other animals that hide or are unapproachable.

Those mother birds! Where do they learn it? It's astounding when you think about their role in the family. The dads are hunters and gatherers and providers in most cases, but the mother is primary. Without her there are no eggs, no chicks, and no ongoing life.

I would never demean the father's role in any family. But I have to tell you, when I watch those mother birds and the way they take their place in nature with dignity and competence, I am overwhelmed with admiration. They keep it together. They maintain the daily schedule. They have no complaints except when dad slips up or a scavenger ruffles their feathers. Then watch out!

I learned to watch birds from my mother. She would say to me, "Son, the mother birds can teach you everything you need to know about courage, fortitude, and commitment. The mother bird's love for her chicks is a perfect metaphor of Yahweh's love for us. Watch the mother and learn of Yahweh."

In the society and culture of my time, women in general were second class. But in the home, in the nest of the family, the mother's power was recognized. I noticed how my mother manifested the qualities she taught me to look for in the birds. I learned of Yahweh's love for us from her. That understanding empowered me to respect every woman. I had a soft spot for all of them, especially the mothers.

MOTHER-IN-LAW: I'M HUNGRY

Jesus entered Peter's house and found Peter's mother-in-law in bed with a fever. He took her by the hand and the fever left her. She got up at once and began to wait on him. Matthew 8:14-15

I could see in her a wisdom that comes from understanding human nature. I liked Peter's mother-in-law from the moment I met her. She knew when to speak up and when to hold back. She was a woman who knew all about boundaries and consequences. Unlike her son-in-law, who lacked interpersonal boundaries and filters, she could see the big picture. She picked her battles. She didn't need to be right all the time, as Peter did.

I knew right away that she was the rock of Peter's family. She held them all together in her quiet, steady way. She liked me, too; I could tell. She sized me up with one quick scan. She could sniff out a phony in two seconds. I passed her sniff test and smiled because I understood her desire to see the truth.

That's why I took her hand, so hot with fever, and helped her sit up, healed. Without a word, but with a look of fulfilled expectation, she got up and asked if anyone was hungry.

"I am!" I said.

MRS. ZEBEDEE: A SMALL FAVOR

The mother of Zebedee's sons came up to him accompanied by her sons, to do him homage and ask of him a favor. "What is it you want?" he said. She answered, "Promise me that these sons of mine will sit, one at your right hand and the other at your left, in your kingdom" In reply Jesus said, "You do not know what you are asking. Can you drink of the cup I am to drink of?" "We can," they said. He told them: "From the cup I drink of, you shall drink. But sitting at my right hand or my left is not mine to give. That is for those to whom it has been reserved by my Father." Matthew 20:20-23

I could see in her a mother's pride for having raised two strong, handsome sons. Her heart was filled with happiness that their lives were prosperous, and that I had chosen them to follow me. She saw the crowds, the miracles, and the adoration of the people who were healed. What mother doesn't want her children's success? What parent doesn't want the peace that comes from seeing a child mature and established in the world?

She is a grateful mother. She knows how fragile life is; how unpredictable and uncontrollable. The mother of James and John felt that her sons deserved honored spots in my kingdom. And she knew I could make it happen for them. So she asked me for a favor. She wanted me to promise that her sons would sit on either side of me in my kingdom. "Oh, mother," I said to her somewhat sadly, "You have no idea what you are asking for. You have no clue what I am going to suffer for the sake of my kingdom." I sighed and shook my head as a chill went down my spine. I knew what was coming, but she did not.

She thought the kingdom was already here, that it was all about loaves and fishes, cures, and miracles. But I knew better. It was best that she did not know what was coming.

I asked her sons if they could drink from the same cup that was waiting for me. They said 'Yes!' immediately, of course. Their mother beamed. None of them had the slightest inkling of the horrible, bitter suffering in that cup. My heart sank because I knew they would indeed be drinking from the same cup coming my way, and that neither they nor their mother would be grateful to me when that time came.

So that their mother could hear, I said, "Don't worry, you will drink from the same cup as I." Their mother again smiled that universal glow of a mother's pride. Then the other shoe dropped when I said, "But I'm not the one who decides who sits beside me in the kingdom. That decision will be made by my Father."

I could see the wheels turning in her head as her face fell in disappointment. She was thinking, *Who is he trying to fool by saying it's not up to him? He is the most powerful man I've ever seen. Everyone loves him! My sons deserve to sit beside him. I'm not asking for a miracle or a cure, after all. I've never seen Jesus side-step a request before. And from a mother, no less!*

Our eyes met. I saw her doubt. Yet, I smiled at her because I also saw her loyalty to her sons, James and John. She would stand by them when the dark days came. It would be a far different favor she would ask of me then.

NAMELESS PROSTITUE: Sweet Smell of Forgiveness

There was a certain Pharisee who invited Jesus to dine with him. Jesus went to the Pharisee's home and reclined to eat. A woman known in the town to be a sinner learned that he was dining in the Pharisee's home. She brought in a vase of perfumed oil and stood behind him at his feet, weeping so that her tears fell upon his feet. Then she wiped them with her hair, kissing them and perfuming them with the oil. When his host, the Pharisee, saw this, he said to himself, "If this man were a prophet, he would know who and what sort of woman this is that touches him – that she is a sinner." In answer to his thought, Jesus said to him, "Simon, I have something to propose to you." "Teacher," he said, "speak."

"Two men owed money to a certain money-lender; one owed a total of five hundred coins, the other fifty. Since neither was able to repay, he wrote off both debts. Which of them was more grateful to him?" Simon answered, "He, I presume, to whom he remitted the larger sum." Jesus said to him, "You are right."

Turning then to the woman, he said to Simon, "You see this woman? I came to your home and you provided me with no water for my feet. She has washed my feet with her tears and wiped them with her hair. You gave me no kiss, but she has not ceased kissing my feet since I entered. You did not anoint my head with oil, but she has anointed my feet with perfume. I tell you, that is why her many sins are forgiven—because of her great love. Little is forgiven the one whose love is small."

He said to her then, "Your sins are forgiven…your faith has been your salvation. Now go in peace." Luke 7:36-48,50

I could see in her the self-awareness of which saints are made. Her fearlessness was born through the labor of necessity. She had come face to face with the sin of selling her body to survive. That's not the way my Father intended life to be lived. And she knew it. But she was trapped in a vise of poverty that kept her scratching the earth like a desperate animal.

But when I looked into her eyes with compassion, and directly to her soul with love, she knew who she was, at last. For the first time in her life she was recognized and acknowledged as a person worthy of respect no matter what she had done in the past, no matter what had brought her to this moment.

I could read her thoughts as clearly as I had read the thoughts of my Pharisee host. *At last! At last!* she was singing with weightless joy, *Someone sees me on the inside and loves me! Loves* **me***!* Her thoughts were dancing and sparkling in her spirit as she looked back at me.

What she saw in my eyes was the unconditional love of the Father for her. That she could even recognize this love (I looked into the eyes of hundreds of people every day) testified to her enormous capacity to give.

So when she dropped to the ground and held my ankles between her hands, and wet my feet with her tears, I knew what she was doing and the meaning of her gesture. And when she poured the sweet-smelling oil on my feet and kissed them and wiped them with her long, dark hair, many in the room had no idea what was happening. Only those who had paid her for their pleasure began to snicker at the sight. Half thought me a fool for not recognizing the town prostitute and the other half presumed she was seducing me for a conquest of her own. They were envious and aroused at the sight of her tender attention toward me.

But she didn't care what they thought, and neither did I. My host, Simon, was one of those who wondered how I could be called a prophet and not know who this woman was who washed my feet with her tears. I knew what Simon was thinking just as surely as I knew this woman's thoughts, so I lifted my head and looked directly at Simon, as though to answer his unspoken question. His eyes blinked in embarrassment because he knew I heard his thoughts as clearly as if they had been spoken aloud.

I said to him, "Little is forgiven the one whose love is small. You claim to love me but I came into your home and you offered me no water for my feet; she has washed my feet with her tears. You did not greet me with a kiss; she has not stopped kissing my feet since I sat down. You did not anoint my head with oil; she has anointed my feet with the finest perfume that has filled your house with its scent. Look at her love, Simon! Her forgiveness is immense because her love is immense. As I said, little is forgiven the one who loves little."

Then I looked down again at this astonishing, beautiful woman with the heart of incomparable gratitude and confirmed what she already knew, "Your sins are forgiven; your faith has healed you. Now you can go in peace." She shall remain nameless although her story will be told forever.

NEAR THE CROSS: PARTING GIFTS

Near the cross of Jesus there stood his mother, his mother's sister, Mary the wife of Clopas, and Mary Magdalene. Seeing his mother there with the disciple whom he loved, Jesus said to his mother, "Woman, there is your son." In turn he said to the disciple, "There is your mother." John 19:25-27

I could barely see her through the blood and dirt crusting around my eyes. But I knew she was there as she had always been since I was born. This woman…how did I get so lucky to have her for my mother? God picked the best for me. And I needed to have the best to prepare me for the troubles I would face in my life. I didn't want her to suffer because of my fate. Yet here she was, her own soul in agony at the sight of me dying before her eyes. Only my mother and her closest women friends dared come so close to me. Only these brave women, who loved her as much as they loved me, showed a fearless loyalty to us both in spite of the danger that surrounded them.

And John, my loving friend, the one without bravado, the one who was gentle and whose exceptional love for me was visible and deep. Only John was right there in the open, not caring what happened to him, only wanting to be close to me—as always, even now.

As I felt my body shutting down I knew the time had come to say goodbye to these special ones whom I loved and to whom I was so grateful. They had given their hearts to me. The least I could do was to make sure my love and loyalty remained alive when I was no longer here to love them myself. What would be the point of my life if our love for each other ended with my death? So with my last breath I gave my mother her destiny: to see me in every person and to be the mother to them that she was to me. She was to love her son in everyone, forever. Her love was that immense, that eternal, like God.

"Woman, behold your son," I whispered, so weak was I at that moment. I was confirming her eternal role as mother: *You are to see me and love me forevermore in my friends. These are your children now. Give to them the same love and care and commitment you gave to me.*

And to my beloved John I confirmed the gift of my mother to him and to all persons in future times: "Son, behold your mother." I wanted John to hear in those four words: *This wonderful mother of mine is your mother from this day forward. She is my gift to the ages. This woman gave me life; now she will show you the way to me.*

That was the greatest act of my entire life; it was greater than the miracles, than the healings, the teaching, the preaching. She was my gift to the world. And then I closed my eyes, exhaled one last time, and felt my body die. All finished now. Complete.

NEW MOM'S JOY: NO ONE CAN TAKE IT FROM YOU

When a woman is about to give birth, she is in great pain. But after it is all over, she forgets the pain and is happy, because she has brought a child into the world. [22] You are now very sad. But later I will see you, and you will be so happy that no one will be able to change the way you feel. John 16:21-22 (Contemporary English Version (CEV))

I could see in the new mother's face a joy I knew I would never totally comprehend. She looked down at the baby in her arms as though she possessed the greatest, most exquisite gift in the world. Her whole body was radiant with love. Childbirth was a deep mystery to me growing up. It was exclusively a woman's experience the way her stomach grew bigger and bigger until the time came for her to give birth.

When I was growing up in Nazareth my mother was one of the women who were called upon when it was getting close to a baby's arrival. It didn't matter what time of the day or night the word came to her through an anxious father or a sibling. She finished up whatever she was doing and hurried off to help the other women in her group.

Only the women were allowed near the mother during labor. The men were just as happy to be left out. The terrifying sounds of screaming and moaning hour after hour sent the men as far from the birthing process as possible. They could handle the births of sheep and cows and camels, but not their own children. It was too overwhelming to helplessly stand by and listen to the agonizing pain of labor coming from their wives.

But when the waiting ended and the family was called in, there before our eyes was a smiling mother with a newborn in her arms. She was happy! I always wondered how that was possible, when just a short time ago she was in agony. How could she switch from sounding close to death to being radiant with happiness? How can that be?

I asked my mother about this. She never dismissed my questions about life's mysteries. Even though she confirmed that only women could understand the workings of the female body, she likened childbirth to the great mystery of sadness and happiness. "Many sad things happen in life," she said, "but when you come through them you appreciate the happy times all the more. No woman looks forward to the pain she must endure in giving birth, but when she sees the face of the little one to whom she has given life, she forgets about the hard work of childbirth and simply rejoices that it's over and she has her baby."

That made sense to me when she put it in the context of loss and gain, pain and happiness, struggle and reward. From that time forward, whenever I heard the cries of a woman in labor I'd think, *Don't worry, mother. You are in misery for a time, but you will forget your pain when you see your baby. Your heart will rejoice with a joy that no one can take from you.*

What a great metaphor to explain what it's like when you are reunited with someone you thought you'd never see again, I thought. *I will use this example to comfort my disciples when they begin to feel the pain of losing me. They will need to understand that their pain will end, and I will return to them, as though reborn. Then all of us will celebrate.*

PARTY AT MARTHA'S: FAREWELL TO FRIENDS

Six days before Passover Jesus came to Bethany, the village of Lazarus whom Jesus had raised from the dead. There they gave him a banquet, at which Martha served. Lazarus was one of those at table with him. Mary brought a pound of costly perfume made from genuine aromatic nard, with which she anointed Jesus' feet. Then she dried his feet with her hair, and the house was filled with the ointment's fragrance. Judas Iscariot, one of his disciples (the one about to hand him over), protested: "Why was not this perfume sold? It could have brought three hundred silver pieces, and the money have been given to the poor." (He did not say this out of concern for the poor, but because he was a thief. He held the purse, and used to help himself to what was deposited there.) To this Jesus replied: "Leave her alone. Let her keep it against the day they prepare me for burial." John 12:1-7

I could see in her a depth of gratitude that no words came close to expressing. "Thanks" is so pitifully inadequate at times, times like these. Mary's depth of loss and grief were bottomless when her brother Lazarus died. Mary knew I loved Lazarus but she had not understood why I stayed away when he got sick. She knew if I had come right away I would not have let him die. "If you had been here he wouldn't have died," she moaned with regret on that dreadful day.

It's one thing to cure leprosy, and another thing to make the blind see or the crippled walk. These are signs of a power far beyond anything humanly possible. But to bring someone out of the grave after four days—now that was really over the top of anyone's comprehension. It was the only time in my public ministry that I had done something so unbelievable. But I was a loyal friend and a generous human being who could not say no to the women whose depths were so like my own. I saw myself in Mary's eyes and in Martha's living smile. So when these sisters threw a party for me the week before my arrest and execution, I welcomed the chance to celebrate with my friends and bask in their gratitude.

When Mary brought out her expensive perfume, she looked in my eyes for a brief second. Her eyes were asking, *Please let me do this for you. I have no words, but I have my lovely, perfumed ointment and my soft hair and my tender hands. I so want to show you in this gesture what I cannot say with words. Please let me.*

How could I say no to her expression of love? She wanted to rub my feet with expensive nard and dry them with her hair. This was the same perfume Mary would bring to my empty tomb in another week, intending to anoint my lifeless body before its burial. But that would be unnecessary, I knew, so I told Judas she was preparing me for my funeral. I knew Judas would grumble at the extravagance of the gesture. He saw only his own monetary advantage in everything that concerned me. Judas was all about silver pieces, not love or loyalty or friendship.

This time Martha didn't complain about Mary not helping her in the kitchen. She was manifesting her own extravagant talents by the oven at that moment. Martha was content to watch her sister pamper me. She knew that she too was about to give me a different kind of pleasure from her culinary gifts. Martha waved from the kitchen and smiled. I waved back at my beautiful friend.

I will let them fuss over me, I thought. *I want to enjoy their happiness one last time.*

PREGNANT OR NURSING: Hard Times Ahead

"The women who are pregnant or are nursing at the breast will fare badly in those days! The distress in the land and the wrath against this people will be great." Luke 21:23

A great crowd of people followed him, including women who beat their breasts and lamented over him. Jesus turned to them and said: "Daughters of Jerusalem, do not weep for me. Weep for yourselves and for your children. The days are coming when they will say, 'Happy are the sterile, the wombs that never bore and the breasts that never nursed.'" Luke 23:27-29

I could see how hard it was going to be for them in times to come during earthquakes, famines, plagues and wars. The women always suffered most, especially those who were pregnant or nursing their babies. The most vulnerable women and children lost far more than anyone else during natural disasters as well as in those catastrophes caused by men. Why is it that the gender which conceives and gives birth to the next generation, feeds them and cares for them throughout their lives ends up powerless and defenseless? Why is that?

They were so good to me, these women, so faithful. I wished they did not have to see me like this, on my way to be executed. I could see in their eyes a mother's loss, her sense of failure at not being able to change the course her child was traveling. What could I say to them? What was left to be said now? And yet I could not pass them without some word to acknowledge their love and loyalty to me. My face was bloody from the thorns in my scalp and my lips were swollen from the soldiers' beatings. But when I saw them weeping desperately at the sight of me I tried to tell them not to cry for me because I knew they would see days sadder than this one. My suffering soon would be over, but they still had hard times ahead when they would consider women who bore no children as the lucky ones.

PSYCHIC WIFE: BAD DREAM

While [Pilate] was still presiding on the bench, his wife sent him a message: 'Do not interfere in the case of that holy man. I had a dream about him today which has greatly upset me.' Matthew 27:19

I could see in her a gift not given to many. In her soul, the veil between conscious and subconscious was almost transparent, similar to me, except that within my being there was no veil at all. She had a special sense of perception, this Governor's wife, the gentile who knew nothing of Yahweh and the faith of his people. And yet she honored Yahweh by accepting her gift and using it to help others she knew.

It's a good thing she was not one of the Chosen People because, as a woman, there is no way she would have been allowed to express her psychic ability in public or private. More than that, had she been a Jew, she might have been stoned to death for practicing sorcery.

But Pilate's wife was surprisingly different. She respected her ability to intuit the lives of people on a psychic level, a power unavailable to most.

I knew about her women's groups. She and her friends met weekly to socialize and share gossip of Herod's kingdom. These were wives of the wealthy who did not have to bake or clean or enter the marketplace. They had time and freedom on their hands. Pilate's wife hosted these weekly gatherings. King Herod's wife, Herodias, attended the group only once. When the psychic looked right through her and asked the king's wife if she was seeking truth, Herodias stood up without saying a word and left the room.

My own ability to hear unspoken thoughts was not known to everyone, but my disciples knew I could read their minds. Most of the time I paid no attention to their mental wanderings. But I was always alert to intensity and intuitive energy around me.

I remember clearly the day when I sensed a woman in the crowd whose energy was calling to me. But it was not that woman herself who was curious; it was the one who sent her to check me out whose energy I felt coming through. When I looked directly into the eyes of the messenger, she was so shocked she quickly turned and left the crowd. *I know who you are* I said to Pilate's wife in my mind. And she heard me, although she did not know where the words she heard were coming from.

When the messenger returned to Pilate's wife, shaken, she relayed how my eyes caught hers in the crowd and seemed to look directly into her soul. Then Pilate's wife knew where the words, *I know who you are*, had come from. They came from my mind to hers.

From that day on I was in her thoughts frequently, both waking and sleeping. She didn't deliberately think about me but her energy attracted my own. Her decency and kindness were magnets to my heart. I knew she reached out to others who were confused or who needed support.

I liked Pilate's wife. She was not afraid of her gifts and she shared her talents with her friends. The men, of course, had nothing to do with her and thought she was a witch of some sort. Another reason they didn't want to be near her was because she knew their hearts and behaviors, which they preferred to keep hidden.

On the night that my friend, Judas, betrayed me, as I cried out to God in agony to spare me from the death I knew was coming, my tortured prayers penetrated the sleep of Pilate's wife. She woke up in a sweat and did not know why.

Later that morning she heard shouting crowds outside the palace and the voice of her husband attempting to reason with an angry mob. She looked through the curtain to the balcony and saw me standing by Pilate. She had never seen me in person, but even if she had she would not have recognized the man she saw standing there shackled, beaten up, face dripping with blood from the thorny crown embedded in his scalp.

She knew it was me because the same frantic, psychic anxiety that woke her up a few hours earlier was again screaming through her being. At that moment she understood what her dream was about. Quickly she summoned a servant to relay a message to Pilate: "Do not interfere in the case of that holy man. I had a dream about him today which has greatly upset me."

But the wives of politicians do not have nearly the same power to sway the minds of their husbands as does a mob about to revolt. Pilate listened to the message from his wife and did what he thought was best: he gave the OK for my execution and went back to his business.

She did what she could for me. She tried. But after that day her psychic energy dulled and her dreams were empty.

QUEEN'S CURIOSITY: THE NEED TO SEE FOR HERSELF

The Queen of the South will rise at the judgment along with the men of this generation and she will condemn them. She came from the farthest corner of the world to listen to the wisdom of Solomon, but you have a greater than Solomon here. Luke 11:31

The queen of Sheba, having heard of Solomon's fame, came to test him with subtle questions. She arrived in Jerusalem with a very numerous retinue, and with camels bearing spices, a large amount of gold, and precious stones. She came to Solomon and questioned him on every subject in which she was interested. King Solomon explained everything she asked about and there remained nothing hidden from him that he could not explain to her. 1Kings 10:1-10

I could see in the Queen of Sheba the desire for truth. She was more than just a pretty face. She was aware that wealth and wisdom are rarely compatible. More often, she knew that the power of wealth led to lust for more power and more wealth. She heard that Solomon was different; that he possessed and expressed qualities that were not ordinarily associated with wealth and power. The Queen wanted to see for herself what this man Solomon was like. She was curious to discover the truth about him.

What I *liked* about her was that she didn't automatically believe everything she heard. She wanted her own experience. She thought for herself and made her own judgments. What I *loved* about her was her ability to recognize genuine godlike greatness underneath the outer trappings of what the world admired.

She wanted the truth.

She had the self-confidence of one who was gifted and godlike. She hoped to recognize in Solomon the blessings of her own heart.

What I was trying to tell the men around me that day was that she would rise up to judge them on the last day because she would not see in them a mirror of her own soul. There would be no reflection of God's love and power and mercy and wisdom in them when they appeared with her before God, as there would be in her.

I was hoping that my followers would be like the Queen of Sheba; that they would want only to recognize for themselves that everything they had heard about me was true. I wanted them to see in me a reflection of my Father in their own hearts, just like the Queen of Sheba saw in Solomon.

I have to see for myself, she thought. She accepted the responsibility to pack up and go see him. She refused to blindly accept the opinions and judgments of others. She had a mind of her own and an uncommon desire for truth, unusual for a queen who had all the outer signs of comfort and wealth.

Yet she was a seeker. That's what I saw in her. She was looking for something that was beyond fine clothes and gold and servants and physical beauty. She wanted more, and wondered what it was about Solomon's reputation that attracted her.

She reminded me of my mother on one level. My mother shared the Queen's thirst for truth. When my mother was told by the angel (I love that story!) that her cousin Elizabeth was pregnant with the great prophet John, she left home immediately to go see her. My mother was around the age of 15 or 16, but even then she let nothing hold her back: not her age, her gender, her circumstances or her social status. That's who I recognized in the Queen of Sheba. My mother is that Queen. All good women are queens to me.

RUTH: FOUND IT!

"What woman, if she has ten silver pieces and loses one, does not light a lamp and sweep the house in a diligent search until she has retrieved what she lost? And when she finds it, she calls in her friends and neighbors to say, 'Rejoice with me! I have found the silver piece I lost.'" Luke 15:8-9

I could see in her the thrill of victory. It's a great feeling to beat the odds and celebrate the win. When I was thirteen or fourteen I didn't understand the meaning of fortitude or determination or grit. But I witnessed it in my own home, and the memory stayed with me for the rest of my life. I even used her as an example when I started to teach publicly many years later.

The day it happened was like most other days. My mother was gathering ingredients to bake bread. I was helping my father in his shop. We both stopped suddenly and looked at each other when we heard a woman's voice shrieking. We couldn't tell at first if there had been an accident or a fire or what. We could not hear the words our neighbor was screaming, only a definite, high-pitched excitement. It was my mother's best friend, Ruth. It was so unlike the wife of Phillip to shriek like that. Then our anxiety increased even more when we recognized the same level of energy in my mother's voice.

We ran to the house to see what was wrong. We expected to find the women in tears and heartbroken. Instead, we froze in bewilderment when we entered the kitchen. There was my mother and Ruth holding each other's hands and jumping up and down in a circle around the bread table. It took a few seconds for our adrenaline to calm down and to comprehend what in the world they were doing, and why. Both of them were dancing and cheering and praising God. Once again, we looked at each other for guidance. We still didn't know what to do.

Finally, they seemed to have worn themselves out. They stopped jumping and held each other close. Then they started to cry. That was the last straw for my father. He took my arm and led me out of the kitchen with a simple, "Let's get out of here." I was completely confused by the whole experience.

When we ate my mother's delicious bread at our meal later that evening, I asked her what had happened to Ruth and why she acted the way she did. My father didn't say a word, but I knew he wanted to know as much as I did. "Oh!" she responded, "What a great day it was for Ruth! A week ago she told me that her toddler had found the box where she and Phillip keep their silver coins. They've been saving for more than a year to purchase a sturdy garden plow. They had taken the box from its safe place because they finally had saved enough for the purchase. But the baby got into the box and had taken the coins to play with. Ruth was beside herself with anxiety when she found the empty box and a trail of silver coins all over the house. She found all but one by that evening. But without the last coin they could not purchase the plow. She told me what had happened and we both agreed to pray to Yahweh for the return of that last coin."

My father and I were mesmerized by the story. My mother had a way with words. After a bite of bread she continued, "You know Ruth when she makes up her mind. She's a strong woman. I wish I had her determination. Anyway, she said to me, 'Mary, I know the coin is somewhere in that house. If I have to sweep every corner ten times, and turn over every stone in the garden, that's what I will do. But I am going to search day and night until I find that coin, if it's the last thing I do!'"

At that point my father and I knew what all the shouting and celebrating was about. After a week of non-stop sweeping and searching, the coin was found in the garden, near the grape vine. Ruth's joy could not be contained, and neither could my mother's. Ruth did not give up. She was determined to find that single coin. And when she did, she and her best friend exploded with glee.

We both were happy for the two friends. I could see pride in my father's eyes for his wife. The next day we talked about Ruth's celebration of her success over finding one simple coin. I didn't really understand how a single coin was worth all the cheering and dancing, but my father said I'd get it one day.

I asked him about the tears they shed in each other's arms after the cheering. Why were they crying if they were happy one minute ago? He responded, "Son, the tears of a woman are beyond a man's power to understand or explain."

SALOME: THE QUIET ONE

There were also women present looking on from a distance.
Among them were Mary Magdalene, Mary the mother of James the
younger and Joses, and Salome. These women had followed Jesus
when he was in Galilee and attended to his needs.

When the Sabbath was over, Mary Magdalene, Mary the mother of
James, and Salome bought perfumed oils with which they intended
to go and anoint Jesus. Very early, just after sunrise, on the first
day of the week they came to the tomb. They were saying to one
another, "Who will roll back the stone for us from the entrance to
the tomb?" Mark 15:40-41;16:1-3

I could see in her a woman of integrity and grace. Salome was a
behind-the-scenes type of person, someone you barely noticed but
who was essential to the functioning of a group. She was practical
and dependable. A natural planner, she could see the big picture
and anticipate what needed to be arranged or purchased ahead of
time so that everything occurred smoothly.

I used to watch Salome without her knowing. She blended in with
her women friends whose names are more familiar: Mary
Magdalene, Mary the mother of James, Martha and Mary. If I had
to compare her with other women in my life, I'd have to say that
Salome was more like Martha than she was like Mary. But unlike
Martha, Salome was not a take-charge person; no, she was the
dependable second-in-command. She didn't need to be the boss. In
fact, she didn't want to be; she preferred the freedom to operate
behind the leader and take pride in pulling off another successful
plan.

At the height of my preaching career, it was no easy task to keep
up with me. My disciples and I were on the road constantly. We

had no headquarters, no base of operation, unless you consider Jerusalem central to our lives as Jews. We moved from town to town, walking hundreds of miles as we crisscrossed Israel. It was the women who anticipated where we should stop along the way and who created a network of contacts for us.

They made sure our group was housed and fed wherever we went. In spite of the growing crowds who were constantly surrounding us, the women were experts at anticipating and fulfilling our needs for nourishment, shelter, and rest.

As months turned into years, Salome was there in the background, caring for me and those who followed me. My lifestyle was itinerant and insecure. It meant that Salome's life also was an anomaly in our society. But she stuck with me. She loved the challenge as much as she loved me.

When my life was taken so violently, Salome was there. On the morning of my resurrection, Salome bought perfumed oils to anoint the body she expected to find in the tomb.

She was there.

She was there when the angel frightened the women with the news that I had been raised up. She hadn't planned on that!

SAMARITAN WOMAN: HOT AND THIRSTY

He had to pass through Samaria, and his journey brought him to a Samaritan town named Shechem near the plot of land which Jacob had given to his son Joseph. This was the site of Jacob's well. Jesus, tired from his journey, sat down at the well. The hour was about noon. When a Samaritan woman came to draw water, Jesus said to her, "Give me a drink." (His disciples had gone off to the town to buy provisions.) The Samaritan woman said to him, "You are a Jew. How can you ask me, a Samaritan and a woman, for a drink?" (Recall that Jews have nothing to do with Samaritans.)

Jesus replied: "If only you recognized God's gift, and who it is that is asking you for a drink, you would have asked him instead, and he would have given you living water."

"Sir," she challenged him, "you do not have a bucket and this well is deep. Where do you expect to get this flowing water? Surely you do not pretend to be greater than our ancestor Jacob, who gave us this well and drank from it with his sons and his flocks?"

Jesus replied: "Everyone who drinks this water will be thirsty again. But whoever drinks the water I give him will never be thirsty; no, the water I give shall become a fountain within him, leaping up to provide eternal life."

The woman said to him, "Give me this water, sir, so that I shall not grow thirsty and have to keep coming here to draw water."

He said to her, "Go, call your husband, and then come back here." "I have no husband," replied the woman. "You are right in saying you have no husband!" Jesus exclaimed. "The fact is, you have

103

had five, and the man you are living with now is not your husband. What you said is true." John 4:4-18

I could see in her a no-nonsense approach to life. She was smart and she had grit. It was noon and very hot. I was watching her draw water at Jacob's well as she was watching me watching her.

No words passed between us. We were ethnic opposites, yet we shared a connection there at the well. We both were there for water.

She appreciated the religious significance of the well. Her spirituality was grounded in history and in faith. I liked her.

We both understood there would be no conversation between us. Jews did not speak to Samaritans. In addition, she was a woman. It would be inappropriate for me to speak to her in public. But as I watched her work I saw what she had in her, and I decided to spar with her.

So I broke the rules and said, "Give me a drink." Her head whipped toward me in shock. For a second she froze in place, her hand on the bucket, ready to lower it into the well. She couldn't believe that I, a Jew, had spoken to her, a Samaritan, and a woman no less. It just didn't happen.

But it was only she and I there at the moment. No one was around to scold me or even to witness my bold move. I had committed two indiscretions. First, I spoke to an outcast; second, I spoke to a woman in public. I caught her off guard; that was evident. There was no chance whatsoever that she was expecting to hear me speak directly to her. Nor did she intend to waste any words on me.

As quickly as she had looked at me in angry amazement, she averted her eyes so as not to commit her own social sin of looking directly at a man in public. I was trying hard not to smile. That would have ruined the seriousness of the encounter, and I wanted to draw something from her heart more than I wanted her to draw water for me from the well. I was there to give her a refreshing spiritual drink.

There was no need for me to repeat my request. We both knew she heard me clearly. It seemed like a long time passed as her mind raced, and she considered her response as she lowered her bucket into the well.

I knew she wouldn't stay silent. I waited for her to challenge me. I loved it when women challenged me. The men were so cerebral and law-oriented when they confronted me and tried to trap me. The women, however, were life-oriented and practical. They made connections with common sense and real life. They were the doers in my culture, the ones who were appreciated as heart and soul of the family infrastructure even though the same culture did not encourage their public contribution. But I did.

As thirsty as I was, I waited for her to make the next move. I was more thirsty for her response. I was willing to wait.

She was up for it. I loved her spunk already. I could see her trying hard not to speak even though she was annoyed that I had spoken to her and wanted her to wait on me. Her physical demeanor had its own language. She wanted me to have to speak again but I did not take my eyes from her or say another word. It was a standoff of sorts.

At last she caved. I knew she couldn't stay silent.

She didn't respond to my need for a drink of water. Rather she reminded me that Jews thought themselves too good to speak to Samaritans. And what was I thinking, speaking to a woman in public? She was wondering who I thought I was, breaking religious, social, and cultural rules like some heathen.

"You are a Jew. How can you ask me, a Samaritan and a woman, for a drink?" She was more or less asking, *What do you really want?*

I loved the way she got right to the point. I could see that in her. She didn't mince words. She was speaking the obvious, not refusing me a drink, but calling me out for my inappropriate behavior. She wouldn't refuse my demand outright, but she could let me know that I was displaying bad manners to be talking to her at all.

I couldn't hold back a smile then. She continued to work the bucket without looking at me. The ball was in my court. So I threw her a curve. She was speaking to me with challenging words so I took it to another level to see if she would meet me there. I said to her, "If only you recognized God's gift, and who it is that is asking you for a drink, you would have asked him instead, and he would have given you living water."

She took the bait. Her practical mind kicked in, as did her fearless tongue. Once again she pointed out the obvious: I had no bucket and no rope. How did I think I was going to get water for her? Where is this 'living water' going to come from, she wanted to know.

And then she really let me have it. In so many words (very few, in fact) she jabbed me with a reminder that 'our' ancestor Jacob had given the well to *her* people and drank from it himself. Was I claiming to be greater than Jacob, she demanded. Did I have my own well? By now she was getting a little testy.

As I said, the woman knew her history and the religious meaning of the well at which we both sat. But I wouldn't let our exchange become a battle. Once more I tried to entice her to another level of faith, into the symbolic meaning of cool, refreshing water that is always available for quenching the strongest thirst. So I said,

"Everyone who drinks this water will be thirsty again. But whoever drinks the water I give him will never be thirsty; no, the water I give shall become a fountain within him, leaping up to provide eternal life."

Now I had her attention! She totally got the concept of water so plentiful and convenient that trudging out to the well would be unnecessary. *What a treat that would be*, she thought.

"I'm in!" she shouted, no longer concerned about manners or societal expectations. "Give me this water, Sir, so that I won't ever be thirsty again and have to drag myself in the heat to this well to get it."

At that moment I knew I had lost the game. She took my words literally. She couldn't get beyond buckets and wells and water and thirst. She worked hard and was tired. She had come to get a bucket of water on a hot day and here comes this brazen Jew talking about never again being thirsty, and with stories about water bubbling up from a fountain of living water. It was too hot to be speaking in parables.

I changed the subject and talked about things in her personal life that I had no way of knowing about because only she and God knew them. I told her to go get her husband and she told me she didn't have one. "True," I said, "in fact you've had five." Once again she looked at me with the same shocked expression. She wondered how I could know about her private life. At that moment she saw in my eyes that I knew everything about her, and who she was inside. Then she got so excited she left her bucket and ran back to town to tell folks about me.

I had to get my own drink.

SARAH: BRIDESMAID

The reign of God can be likened to ten bridesmaids who took their torches and went out to welcome the groom. Five of them were foolish while the other five were sensible. The foolish ones, in taking their torches, brought no oil along, but the sensible ones took flasks of oil as well as their torches. The groom delayed his coming, so the bridesmaids began to nod, then to fall asleep. At midnight someone shouted, 'The groom is here! Come out and greet him!' At the outcry all the virgins woke up and got their torches ready. The foolish ones said to the sensible, 'Give us some of your oil. Our torches are going out.' But the sensible ones replied, 'No, there may not be enough for you and us. You had better go to the dealers and buy yourself some.' While they went off to buy it the groom arrived, and the ones who were ready went in to the wedding with him. Then the door was barred. Later the other bridesmaids came back. 'Master, master,' they cried. 'Open the door for us.' But he answered, 'I tell you I do not know you.'
Matthew 25:1-12

I could see in Sarah the pain of disappointment and rejection. I felt sorry for Ruth's daughter, our neighbor growing up. It was Ruth who danced around the kitchen with my mother when she found the coin she had lost.

Ruth's daughter, Sarah, had been invited to be a bridesmaid in the wedding of her girlfriend. As I understood the story, retold to me by my mother, the bridesmaids were on watch for the bridegroom, as is typical in our tradition. They were told he would arrive by 7:00 PM, but he didn't show up until midnight. The bridesmaids had fallen asleep and left their torches burning. By midnight every torch had burned out.

Several of the bridesmaids had brought extra oil with them. They had been in other weddings, and knew that the partying groom and his groomsmen often did not show up when they said they would. Sarah, however, expected the groom to show up at 7:00 PM, as planned. She had enough oil to last until 9:00 and did not think it was necessary to bring extra oil for her torch.

I watched my mother and Ruth comfort Sarah. I wanted to comfort her, too, but I had no idea what I could do. I was a teenager with no experience of crying bridesmaids. At that time in my life women were an intimidating mystery to me.

So I tried to understand the situation logically: I thought about the balance between expectations and reality; about being prepared for the unexpected; about protecting yourself from all possible consequences. But what I could not deal with was the tears of a bridesmaid who had her heart broken. What can be said or done when that happens?

I never forgot that experience of helplessness, of knowing there was nothing I could do. I hoped that someday I could turn the story into a parable that would have meaning for someone.

SHOUT OUT FOR MOMS: TEACH YOUR CHILDREN WELL

While he was saying this, a woman from the crowd called out,
"Blest is the womb that bore you and the breasts that nursed you!"
Luke 11:27-28

I could see in her outspoken intelligence the insight and courage I wished my disciples possessed. She had a fearlessness about her that could not be suppressed, not even in our culture where a woman's place was well defined. I had seen her before, her bright eyes and her hunger for the gift of personal freedom I came to give to anyone who wanted it. She wanted it.

Every now and then she would shout out something that annoyed my disciples. They thought she was interrupting me, but I enjoyed her ability to allow herself to say publicly what she was thinking. And she always called out to me as though she had known me since I was a small boy in her village who had played with her son and been in her home. Maybe I had. Maybe I reminded her of her own son, and when she looked at me she experienced that familiarity, that secret communication between mothers and sons.

I caught a glimpse of her sparkling eyes that day when we had stopped to eat in a small town. I smiled inwardly and thought, *Oh good, she will have something to say. I wonder what it will be this time.* Peter saw her, too, and tried to steer me in another direction, but I continued to watch her make her way through the waves of people who came to gawk.

Our eyes connected and I waved to her. She lifted both arms and jumped. I started to chuckle at the sight. Peter rolled his eyes and shook his head back and forth. The woman was obviously

111

delighted that I acknowledged her. She was thinking that I must have been taught to respect women by an exceptional mother.

She was right, of course.

It was my mother who taught me in words and by example to respect every person and to treat everyone the way I wished to be treated. It was my mother who taught me the importance of simple, kind gestures like a wave and a smile.

She was right, of course.

She honored my mother when she shouted out, "Blessed is the womb that bore you and the breasts that nursed you!" She was saying, *What a lucky man you are to have a mother who taught you so well!*

She was right, of course.

SIBLINGS: FAMILY RESTORED

There was a certain man named Lazarus who was sick. He was from Bethany, the village of Mary and her sister Martha. (This Mary whose brother Lazarus was sick was the one who anointed the Lord with perfume and dried his feet with her hair.) The sisters sent word to Jesus to inform him, "Lord, the one you love is sick." Upon hearing this, Jesus said: "This sickness is not to end in death; rather it is for God's glory, that through it the Son of God may be glorified."

Jesus loved Martha and her sister and Lazarus very much. Yet, after hearing that Lazarus was sick, he stayed on where he was for two days more. Finally he said to his disciples, "Let us go back to Judea."

When Jesus arrived at Bethany, he found that Lazarus had already been in the tomb four days....When Martha heard that Jesus was coming she went to meet him, while Mary sat at home. Martha said to Jesus: "Lord, if you had been here, my brother would never have died. Even now, I am sure that God will give you whatever you ask of him"

When Mary came to the place where Jesus was, seeing him, she fell at his feet and said to him, "Lord, if you had been here my brother would never have died." When Jesus saw her weeping and the Jews who had accompanied her also weeping, he was troubled in spirit, moved by the deepest emotions. "Where have you laid him?" he asked. "Lord, come and see," they said. Jesus began to weep, which caused the Jews to remark, "See how much he loved him."

Once again troubled in spirit, Jesus approached the tomb. It was a cave with a stone laid across it. "Take away the stone," Jesus directed. Martha, the dead man's sister, said to him, "Lord, it has been four days now; surely there will be a stench!" Jesus replied, "Did I not assure you that if you believed you would see the glory of God displayed?" They then took away the stone and Jesus looked upward and said, "Father, I thank you for having heard me. I know that you always hear me but I have said this for the sake of the crowd, that they may believe that you sent me."

Having said this he called loudly, "Lazarus, come out!" The dead man came out bound head and foot with linen strips, his face wrapped in a cloth. "Untie him," Jesus told them, "and let him go free." John 11:1-7; 17; 20-22; 32-36; 38-44

I could see in Martha the common human struggle between faith and disappointment. The first thing she said to me was, "If you had been here this never would have happened." She was talking about her brother's death, four days earlier. She was right about that. This was logical, level-headed Martha speaking. If I had come as soon as I received word that Lazarus was sick, I wouldn't have let my good friend die. And his death had now caused unspeakable grief in the hearts of his devoted sisters, whom I also loved like my own family.

She wanted to ask, "Why? Why didn't you come sooner to heal him?" but she didn't. Instead, she opened the door for healing to occur when she said, "Even now I am sure that God will give you whatever you ask of him."

My wonderful Martha! How's that for remarkable faith? She was saying *even now, even after he has been dead for four days, I know that God will give you whatever you ask.* She knew me so much better than my disciples did. She understood my love for her and Mary and Lazarus. She knew who I was and what I could do. She had no doubts about me. She believed in me.

And then Mary came running toward me, grief stricken. She repeated Martha's realization, "If you had been here Lazarus would still be alive." If, if, if only. If only I had been here. If only I had come sooner.

Suddenly it all hit me at once: the loss, the sadness, the grief. My good friend was dead. My heart was breaking. I started to cry. "Where is he?" I choked. I had to do something. Martha's words were filling my head: "Even now, even now." She knew me that well. She took my hand and led me to the cave and looked in my eyes. "Even now...I believe in you" her eyes were saying with assurance. Martha was not asking for a miracle. She was assuring me that in spite of everything her trust in me was complete.

Her reverie was abruptly cracked, however, when I said through my tears, "Take away the stone." Then the sensible, matter-of-fact Martha stepped forward to remind me that a four-day-old dead body would stink. *That's my Martha,* I thought, *Always the realist.* My response to her was, "You took me at my word when I told you that if you believe you will see the glory of God."

And then I looked up to heaven and thanked God for hearing me now, as he always did when I prayed. What I wanted most was that everyone watching would believe that I had been sent to them by him. That was the meaning of everything I did.

The heavy stone was rolled away. I yelled inside, "Lazarus, come out!" There was a palpable silence as the crowd of us stood there, unmoving for at least a minute. And then there was the sound of slow shuffling, feet not walking but dragging. Now the crowd was frozen in place, wanting but not wanting to know what was moving toward the opening of the cave.

When a white-bandaged arm grabbed the edge of the rock opening, everyone screamed! A few people ran away, scared out of their wits. I was worried Lazarus himself might die again—of fright this time—when he finally emerged from his dark slumber and heard the hysteria of his terrified friends.

I glanced at Martha. She was smiling. She looked up at me. Her eyes had that same, solid, unwavering trust. "Unwrap him and let him go free," I said to her. Martha fearlessly approached her brother and hugged him. "Martha, is that you?" asked a voice under the cloth covering the head of the resurrected corpse in white.

"Yes, Lazarus, I'm here. Let's go home."

I could see in her the absolute confidence of one who trusts in me.

SICK CHILD: MOTHERS KNOW

Then Jesus left that place and withdrew to the district of Tyre and Sidon. It happened that a Canaanite woman living in that locality presented herself, crying out to him, "Lord, Son of David, have pity on me! My daughter is terribly troubled by a demon." He gave her no word of response. His disciples came up and began to entreat him, "Get rid of her. She keeps shouting after us." "My mission is only to the lost sheep of the house of Israel," Jesus replied. She came forward then and did him homage with the plea, "Help me, Lord!" But he answered, "It is not right to take the food of sons and daughters and throw it to the dogs." "Please, Lord," she insisted, "even the dogs eat the leavings that fall from their masters' tables." Jesus then said in reply, "Woman, you have great faith! Your wish will come to pass." That very moment her daughter got better. Matthew 15:21-28

I could see in her a determination to get what she needed for her child. I knew she wouldn't give up until I said yes. She had so much faith, this foreigner, this immigrant, this uneducated, poor woman with the loud voice. The only reason I ignored her was because I knew she wouldn't give up. It was a chance to teach my thickheaded disciples a lesson in what real faith in me means.

I played along with them when they huffed, "Lord, get rid of her. She is annoying us. She won't shut up." I agreed with them by saying, "It's not my job. She's not one of us. I'm not here for the likes of her." Then I smiled because I knew without a doubt that this desperate, faith-filled mother was more my follower than these bigoted men who were more concerned with order than they cared about the needs of people.

She was pushy, too, as mothers can be when a child is sick and needs help immediately. She elbowed her way through layers and layers of people. I don't know how she did it, but mothers are like that. The combination of her dogged determination to speak to me directly, along with her annoying shouts and her rock-solid expectation, I knew it wouldn't be long before she was in my face.

She made it. I could hardly keep from telling her that her daughter was already well. But I let her have her say. She honored God when she believed I could make her child well. "Help me, Lord!" she insisted. Her words were not a plea, but a command. I loved that spark in her. But my disciples were still ready to escort her away from me. I needed to teach them about faith in my power, so I put her off one more time. (I knew it wouldn't matter to her; she wasn't going anywhere until she received from me what she knew I could—and would—give her.)

So I said to her, "Look, the children of the family are fed at the table. *They* deserve the food, not the family dog." I could hear the mumbling of self-righteous agreement from my friends, these followers of mine who still didn't get it, who still felt they were part of an exclusive club whose members were hand-picked. Right on cue she came back at me with a spot-on, perfect retort. "Yes, Lord," she agreed, "but even the family dogs are given the scraps from the table that no one else wants."

She had me then. I wanted to take her in my arms and make her my disciple. I could see Peter thinking over her bold response. I was afraid he and James were going to pick her up by the elbows and drag her out. But they saw me throw my head back and heard me laugh out loud, so they stepped back, confused. I then said to her, "Woman, your faith is astounding! You have what you expected to receive by coming to me."

Then *her* face lit up. She had not the slightest doubt I had healed her child. She knew it in her bones, in her gut and in her heart. She knew she had been right about this Jew, Jesus. She couldn't wait to get home.

SUSANNA: HEALING TOUCH

There was a woman in the area who had been afflicted with a hemorrhage for a dozen years. She had received treatment at the hands of doctors of every sort and exhausted her savings in the process, yet she got no relief; on the contrary, she only grew worse. She had heard about Jesus and came up behind him in the crowd and put her hand to his cloak. "If I just touch his clothing," she thought, "I shall get well." Immediately her flow of blood dried up and the feeling that she was cured of her affliction ran through her whole body. Jesus was conscious at once that healing power had gone out from him. Wheeling about in the crowd, he began to ask, "Who touched my clothing?" His disciples said to him, "You can see how this crowd hems you in, yet you ask, 'Who touched me?'" Despite this he kept looking around to see the woman who had done it. Fearful and beginning to tremble now as she realized what had happened, the woman came and fell in front of him and told him the whole truth. He said to her, "Daughter, it is your faith that has cured you. Go in peace and be free of this illness." Mark 5:25-34

I could see in her the desire to simply slip through the crowd and go back home, now that she was healed. But when I felt the energy being drawn from me I knew that someone special had touched me. And it wasn't even my body that had been touched, it was my cloak. But the faith of this invisible one was enough to draw from me the power to heal her. It was as though she had a magnet that attracted to her the healing energy she knew I had. That could not happen unless the depth of her faith was as certain as my ability to heal her.

Usually the people crowding around me are there for a show or for food. I am caught between my desire to heal the physical problems of everyone who suffers, and my mission to proclaim the healing of the minds and hearts of all who live in this wondrous world. People tend to be more attracted to miracles and phenomena than to the healing powers of love and forgiveness. That's why I always said, "Don't tell anyone" after I healed them. But they don't listen. The first thing they do is go out and shout it from the rooftops. They are so overjoyed to be able to see or walk or watch their dead child sit up and smile. They cannot contain their thrilled gratitude. I can't blame them for wanting to spread the good news, even if my Good News is so much greater than what the senses perceive.

When I felt the healing energy being drawn out of me I thought, *Who is that? Who has this great faith that can draw my healing power through my clothes, even without touching my body?* I twirled around to see who it was. I asked my disciples who touched me. Peter looked at me like I was crazy. He said, "Are you kidding, Lord? We can't even move through this mass of humanity. We are being crushed by this mob, and you're asking who touched you?!"

"Who touched me?!" I shouted out in every direction as I continued to circle in place. I wanted to meet the one with great faith and miraculous expectations. "Who touched me?!" I kept yelling as I gazed at the thousand faces all around me.

And then I saw her. She looked guilty and afraid, like a child caught in a naughty act. She thought I was angry because I kept yelling, "Who touched me?!" But she knew as well as I did that she was the one I was looking for. I was happy for her and I wanted to meet her. I joyfully waved to her to come back. She looked relieved when she saw me smile.

She courageously described the embarrassing, messy, debilitating bleeding she had endured for the past fifteen years. No man would touch her and her women friends suspected her problem was a punishment for a past sin. They thought maybe she had relations with a married man and this was her consequence.

She knew better, however. She tried every doctor, every herb, every healer, and nothing worked. The blood kept flowing day after day, nonstop. She was getting weaker and needed a power far beyond anything she had tried up until today. And then she heard the stories about this Jew from Nazareth they called Jesus. He was healing blind people. He was casting out demons from the minds of the possessed. He was bringing people back to life who were declared dead. It wasn't hard to conclude that if this man could perform miracles he could stop a bleed.

She had been thinking, *As soon as he touches people they are healed. His energy comes through his body. There's no way I can get his attention, and I surely don't want to tell a man—and certainly not a crowd of strangers—about my constant bleeding. But if I can just get close enough to touch his clothes, that will be enough to draw his amazing healing energy through my skin and into my body that so desperately wants to be healthy again.*

I love these women who are so intuitive. They get it. They understand how energy works. They believe and they push through mobs of people to feel the current, the vibration that channels through me to the world around us. Usually they shout out to me, but this time it was I who was shouting out, "Who touched me?!" They most often think they have to ask me for healing but not this one. She knew my power was there for the taking. She believed it, and her faith in me healed her. That's what I told her: "It is your faith that has cured you." She gladly claimed for herself what I had to give, what she didn't even have to ask for.

TAMAR'S GRIEF: Loss and Return

*Soon afterward he went to a town called Naim, and his disciples
and a large crowd accompanied him. As he approached the gate of
the town a dead man was being carried out, the only son of a
widowed mother. A considerable crowd of townsfolk were with
her. The Lord was moved with pity upon seeing her and said to
her, "Do not cry." Then he stepped forward and touched the litter;
at this, the bearers halted. He said, "Young man, I bid you get up."
The dead man sat up and began to speak. Then Jesus gave him
back to his mother. Luke 7:11-15*

I could see in her the grief of a parent who has had her heart ripped
out of her chest and buried forever with a dead child. Her name
was Tamar. My own heart began to hurt, physically hurt, as I saw
her walk with those lifeless eyes. I could hardly watch Tamar force
herself take every agonizing step along the last mile to her son's
grave. To make it worse, she was a widow. Now she had no one.
Tamar was totally alone in this world of loss. I thought about the
many parents my mother had consoled in past years, her own tears
for her friends and members of our synagogue whose children had
preceded them in death. My mother had a premonition of what was
waiting for her, and I knew she shed premature tears for her loss
when my time came.

This too touched my deepest spirit—to know that my own mother's
heart would rip with sorrow when she held her only child in her
arms, dead. I had to do something, if only to assure myself that my
mother would believe that death is not the end to love.

I stood there in the road facing the mourners who were walking
toward me. The mother's friends were on either side of her, holding
her up, keeping up with the people of Naim who were there to
grieve with her. My disciples and I were blocking their way now.

Peter was getting nervous, as usual, and was trying to move me out of the road so that the mourners could pass by. But I stood there. Some recognized me and stopped. They looked so defeated. I reached out to the mother, Every Mother, and as I put my hand on Tamar's hand I said, "Don't cry." I was close to tears myself, but I managed to say that much. Then I turned to the bier where her dead son was wrapped in white and surrounded by flowers. I said to him simply, "Young man, you can get up now." And he did. He sat up.

My disciples weren't shocked to see the widow's son sit up. By this time they were used to miracles. They saw them happen every day. What always surprised me, however, was their inability to fathom my compassion, especially for mothers, for women, whose place in society was so repressed and unappreciated. From the depths of my heart I understood a mother's power in her unconditional commitment to her children in love. How could that Godlike commitment not have the power to move my heart?

The young man began to speak. He was struggling to unwrap himself from his death shroud and wanted to know what was going on. I helped him stand up and gave him back to his mother. She, too, had come back to life.

WATCHING HER BAKE: THE MIRACLE OF YEAST

"He went on: 'To what shall I compare the reign of God? It is like yeast which a woman took to knead into three measures of flour until the whole mass of dough began to rise.'" Luke 13:20-21

I could see competence in her, the way she gathered her ingredients, measured the flour and then added the yeast and water. "Timing is everything when you bake bread," she used to tell me as I stood there with my chin resting on my folded arms high on the bread table. It was only recently I had grown tall enough to watch her as I stood up rather than having to sit on a stool. I loved being there with her as she baked bread. She made it look easy as she balanced the timing of the oven's heat with the rising bread. It was important that every step be done at the right moment or the bread would not come out perfect. My mother always seemed to get it right.

Once I asked her how she made the dough blow up like a shepherd's tent in the wind. I was captivated by the growth of that dough ball from a thick rock to a puffy feather pillow. I waited patiently until she gave me permission to stick my finger in the spongy mass to let out the air. She wasn't too happy the time I hammered the dough with my fist, so I promised to use only my fingers from then on.

I thought a lot about the miracle of yeast. In comparison with the amount of flour needed, you'd guess the yeast played a minor role. But the yeast was essential to the process. I'm not complaining about unleavened bread, but really there's no comparison between eating unleavened bread and bread made with yeast. Even the smell of the two breads baking is different.

Yeast is like a secret ingredient, like magic. *What's in that stuff, anyway?* I wondered as I watched her. I figured one day I'd come up with a comparison for the amazing properties of yeast. It would have to be something special, something wondrous.

WIDOW OF ZAREPHATH: GOD'S CHOICE

So the Lord said to [Elijah]: 'Move on to Zarephath of Sidon and stay there. I have designated a widow there to provide for you.' 1 Kings 17:8

Indeed, let me remind you, there were many widows in Israel in the days of Elijah when the heavens remained closed for three and half years and a great famine spread over the land. It was to none of these that Elijah was sent, but to a widow of Zarephath near Sidon. Luke 4:25-26

I could see her in my mind when I studied the Hebrew Bible. She fascinated me, not because she was extraordinary, but because she seemed to have been plucked from nowhere. And yet her role was important in the life of the great prophet, Elijah. She wasn't one of the Chosen People; rather, she was very much a gentile foreigner.

Every time that passage was read in the synagogue when I was growing up I wondered, *Why her? Why did Yahweh select her to help Elijah when there were so many Israelites who could have given him more? Why choose a woman and an outsider?*

Every time I read the story in the book of Kings I could see in her the pitiful look of starvation. She expected to die that night with her son because they had barely a handful of flour and a little oil, and nothing more to eat. When Elijah asked her for bread she told him her desperate situation.

I smiled when I thought of Elijah's predicament. The Lord had clearly sent him to this specific widow, in this specific town to stay with and be provided for. But she and her son were starving to death and had not a bite of food to eat.

But Elijah did not doubt Yahweh's word. And the widow did not doubt Elijah's word. Both had been chosen and both responded in faith, despite the unlikely odds of success.

Elijah was a great prophet, and the widow was a nobody. She was a woman alone and destitute. She was a mother who could not provide for her son, and a foreigner to Elijah. Yet Yahweh brought them together for his purposes and both fulfilled his plan.

God had his eye on her. God chooses whom he wills to choose, with seemingly no rhyme or reason. The widow was a symbol. I knew for a long time that I would use her as an example of God's equal love for all people, but also a sign of his heart's love for widows and mothers.

Those who think they've cornered the market on God's favor are in for a surprise. I knew I had a hard road ahead of me to convince the people of my day that Yahweh's love and forgiveness are extended to everyone, even starving gentile widows. When I thought of the widow of Zarephath, I drew strength from her trust and from Yahweh's concern for her human needs.

That's how I'll treat people when my time comes, I said to myself back then.

WIDOW'S DONATION: SHE GAVE ALL

Taking a seat opposite the treasury, he observed the crowd putting money into the collection box. Many of the wealthy put in sizable amounts; but one poor widow came and put in two small copper coins worth a few cents. He called his disciples over and told them: "I want you to observe that this poor widow contributed more than all the others who donated to the treasury. They gave from their surplus wealth, but she gave from her want, all that she had to live on." Mark 12:41-44

I could see in her a feeling of joy that she had something to bring and to pay forward. It wasn't about the money for her, it was about the power she felt in having something to give, no matter how small. So many of her friends had nothing at all to give, or so they thought. They worried and fretted and feared. But not her, I could tell. There was a strength about her that said, *Whether I give two cents or two million cents does not matter to Yahweh. What matters is knowing to the depths of my being that I am giving something back to him with a smiling, grateful heart for all that he has so lovingly given to me. The Lord loves giving good things to me as much as I love giving to Him. I do not worry.*

She was not afraid to be poor, nor resentful of having nothing, nor afraid that she would not have enough. Her trust and expectation of God's providence radiated in her confident face.

I loved sitting there watching folks go in and out of the treasury. I could tell when people gave generously or resentfully. It was so interesting to look into their hearts for their motives and intentions. My own heart jumped when I saw the widow digging in her pockets for something to give as a sign of her loyalty and gratitude. I watched her face as it was transformed from intense concentration mixed with worry, to a look of triumph as her hands came up with two pennies she knew were there somewhere. She walked up with the rich who were offering a small percentage of their profits and gloating over their self-perceived generosity. She, on the other hand, was delighted just to be there with something to give, even if was all she had. There was an important lesson here for my disciples, so I called them over.

WOMAN: YOU ARE FREE

On a Sabbath day he was teaching in one of the synagogues. There was a woman there who for eighteen years had been possessed by a spirit which drained her strength. She was badly stooped—quite incapable of standing erect. When Jesus saw her, he called her to him and said, "Woman, you are free of your infirmity." He laid his hand on her, and immediately she stood up straight and began thanking God. Luke 13:10-13

I could see the weight of the world on her back, and my heart sank at the sight of her deformed and painful existence. She was so disabled she needed a thick and heavy tree branch to hold her up as she shuffled along. Her back was curved to such a degree that she could not lift her head to see what was in front of her. Why she had this burden of body and mind I cannot say. Many accidents of nature occur in an imperfect world.

But I also could see in her a gentleness with herself and with the body that burdened her. I saw her often in the Synagogue where I was teaching. She was there praying for others, asking God to gift them with the health and energy she lacked. Imagine how amazed the angels are by such a prayer—I know I was!

I called to her to come over to me. Leaning on her branch she dragged her body to the place where I was sitting. Everyone around us was watching in electrified silence. The only sound was the slow drag of her feet and the thump of the branch on the tile floor with each step.

She saw only the bottom half of my robes and my feet. She could not raise her head any higher than that. She looked like she was in the process of curling up, but not giving up. Rather, she was giving out strong, determined vibrations which I could feel.

I leaned down and placed my hand on her rounded back. She stiffened. No one had touched her for 18 years. Time stood still as my energy spread through her back and down her spine. She started to shake.

I knew her name but I addressed her in the name of her gender that I so loved: "Woman," I said, "you are free of your suffering." As easily as though it happened every day, natural as could be, she lifted her head, and then her shoulders, and then her back. In slow motion she stood up straight and lifted her face and her eyes heavenward. Her branch dropped to the floor with a thud as she raised her arms in thanks to God. She twirled around and around the floor of the Synagogue, tall and straight, looking above and beyond to a whole new world.

WOMEN WHO LOVED HIM: ATTENTIVE AND FAITHFUL

*Many women *were present looking on from a distance. They had followed Jesus from Galilee to attend to his needs. Among them were Mary Magdalene, and Mary the mother of James and Joseph, and the mother of Zebedee's sons. Matthew 27:55-56*

Meanwhile, Mary Magdalene and Mary the mother of Joses observed where he had been laid. When the Sabbath was over, Mary Magdalene, Mary the mother of James, and Salome bought perfumed oils with which they intended to go and anoint Jesus. Mark 15:47-16:1

*The twelve accompanied him, and also **some women** who had been cured of evil spirits and maladies; Mary called the Magdalene, from whom seven devils had gone out, Joanna, the wife of Herod's steward Chuza, Susanna, and **many others** who were assisting them out of their means. Luke 8:1-3*

*The women were Mary of Magdala, Joanna, and Mary the mother of James. **The other women** with them also told the apostles, but the story seemed like nonsense and they refused to believe them. Luke 24:10-11*

Near the cross of Jesus there stood his mother, his mother's sister, Mary the wife of Clopas, and Mary Magdalene. John 19:25

I loved them all.

Too many to count.

Only a few were named by the gospel writers, and they hesitated even then to name women. Women were second-class citizens, but there were so many who loved me and cared for me and followed me, that they had to be written about and named, if my whole story would be told. The women were as much a part of my story as the men were. The men tried my patience, but never the women. They anticipated my needs and the needs of the men who also followed me.

When I was murdered I didn't have a chance to tell anyone to write my story or to include my women friends in the writing. But the writers knew they had to include the women, in spite of their reluctance to acknowledge their role. Even so, they didn't tell the whole story. They mentioned only ten of my women by name, and even then, only by their relationship to their husband or their sons.

I know what I saw in them, but what did they see in me? What was it about me that drew them to me?

What would they say about me?

Maybe soon they will tell the story of their relationship with me from their own perspectives. I will look forward to reading what they have to say.

~~~~~

The End

About the Author

The roots of my spiritual writing began when I spent seven years living a monastic life in a Trappist religious order in the 1970s. After retiring from a career as a grant writer in 2011, I returned to a daily practice of spiritual reading and writing, and *The Women in His Life* was born. It is my hope that these Gospel-based stories will benefit readers who are searching for a more personal experience of the central figure of the New Testament. The book is unique because these narratives are written from what I imagine to be the thoughts, words, and feelings of Jesus in each situation. I've tried to capture the individuality of the women Jesus interacted with or reflected upon during his life. It is my wish that the reader's spiritual journey will be richer after meditating upon these stories. Christian believers will discover the deep appreciation Jesus has for women of all ages and situations in life. I'm a Pennsylvania native and I've lived in Florida since the mid-1980's where I raised my son. In addition to writing, I enjoy traveling, photography, family, Reiki, and being with friends. Please contact me by email at PatriciaDalyWrites@gmail.com or on my author page at www.PatriciaDalyWrites.com

EXCERPT FROM MY NEXT PUBLICATION

My next publication will be a true short story about hurt, damage, forgiveness and healing. We all have experiences of rejection, misunderstanding, and failure. In *Indelible Imprint* I share the details of a painful experience and the unusual circumstances that contributed to my recovery. It is a story that helped me realize that the way we live in this life impacts not only the life of the soul beyond death, but also the unbreakable connections we have to those whose lives have impacted our own in this life.

~~~

INDELIBLE IMPRINT

One of my favorite books is *Final Payments* by Mary Gordon, published in 1978. It's a novel about being freed from the debt of your damaged past so you can be released from its hold and move on.

Hurt and suffering can end up a double whammy: you suffer the damage, and then you are frustrated by how incapable you are to do anything about it. It isn't even about revenge or payback, but rather, the realization of being powerless. So you carry both a load of grief and a burden of injustice.

How is it possible to heal when the one who hurt you doesn't deserve your forgiveness? The answer is: it's not possible. It takes a miracle.

That miracle happened for me many years after someone I trusted hurt me spiritually and damaged my soul. Like so many of life's punches below the belt, I got my breath back, but not the air that kept my spirit afloat in my solar plexus. My inner, solar power didn't shine as brightly as it once did. The worst part was that for years I didn't realize the breadth of the damage, because I got used to living in the shadow of my pain's abiding scars and painful memories.

In 1970, when I was almost 21-years-old, the place I called home for the next seven years was a Trappistine monastery located in Wrentham, Massachusetts. Mount Saint Mary's Abbey was founded in 1949 and today remains an active community. There are many reasons why a person would choose to live in such a society. When your basic needs are met, without the obligations of making a living, paying bills or taking care of anyone else, your mind and soul are free to tend to spiritual pursuits. I chose it because I felt it was an ideal environment for the spiritual development I yearned for.

The monastic life I'd felt called to, and wanted very much, was a difficult one. It is a life of silence and work following the guidelines of the Rule of St. Benedict which dates back to the 5th Century. The Rule describes the ideals and values of monastic life and is the basis for almost every Christian monastic community in the West up to the present time. Today there are 175 Trappist monasteries around the world (www.ocso.org).

A Trappist monastery is not a democracy. It can't be when your obedience is pledged to God in the person of the community's leader who is the abbot or abbess. You take a vow of obedience to God and in return you trust to receive God's direction through her. She is your spiritual guide as well as the governor of the community. St. Benedict supports the abbot's right to have the last word:

"Whenever an important matter is to be undertaken in the monastery the abbot should call the entire community together and should set forth the agenda. After hearing the various opinions of the brothers, he should consider all and then do what he thinks best...They should leave the question to the abbot's resolution so that they may obey that which he decides is best." (Rule, Chapter 3, The Counsel of the Brothers).

~~~~

End of excerpt

Made in the USA
Coppell, TX
23 March 2023

14658049R00085